CHESHIRE

County of Contrasts

by
J. Brian Curzon

Dalesman Books
1978

£1.60

The Dalesman Publishing Company Ltd.,
Clapham (via Lancaster), North Yorkshire

First published 1978

© J. Brian Curzon, 1978

ISBN: 0 85206 477 2

Printed in Great Britain by
Galava Printing Co. Ltd., Hallam Road, Nelson, Lancashire

Contents

The cover photographs show:- Front: Autumn on the Dee at Chester (S.C. Sedgwick); Back: Moreton Old Hall. Photographs in the text are on pages 49 - 56. All uncredited pictures are by F. Leonard Jackson.

Foreword

EVERYBODY has heard of Cheshire -- if only because of its cats and cheeses. But how many people know the infamous Lady Hamilton was a local lass made bad, that a Cheshire man supplied Shakespeare with plots for his plays or that the county is haunted by the ghost of a headless duck?

In this guide, Mr. Curzon, Cheshire born and bred, sets out to widen the reader's knowledge of the region. No earth shattering new theories will stun the learned local historian but neither will the average person get lost in long-winded academic arguments.

This is the first publication of its kind to deal with Cheshire's historical interest and scenic beauty since local government re-organisation ran amok with the boundaries in April 1974. As such, it should prove of value to both the first-time visitor and to Cheshire residents who want to know more about their home ground. They will certainly find there is more to England's greenest county than cats and cheeses.

The City Unique

CHESHIRE has no great modern industrial cities but in 1975 its county town, the city of Chester, was recognised as one of the most interesting towns in Europe and it was one of the four places in the United Kingdom selected for special consideration in 'European Architectural Heritage Year'.

Each visit to the city shows us a different aspect. No matter how often we come there is something new - something that we have missed before, or a corner that we have not visited. Where else but Chester could there be such a link of old and new, as a Bishop's Palace with a disco in the cellar! Yet we find this at Bishop Lloyd's House, a splendid 17th century building rich with carvings. Pleasing evenings in Chester may be spent visiting the old pubs, each with its own story. The 17th century home of the Chester Heralds—now the *Old King's Head*—has old beams and a fire-place with painted shields of the family and their various marriages. A sword hung behind the bar was uncovered during restoration work. It is conjectured that it was hidden after a crime centuries ago. *The Pied Bull* in Northgate Street has an old fire-place with painted coats of arms and rich oak panels, rare cupboards with pierced designs in which food was stored and a Jacobean staircase. It was from here that George Borrow started out to explore 'Wild Wales'.

The town house of the Earls of Shrewsbury is a pub now, the *Bear and Billet*. It has a fine long window in Tudor style with leaded panes and doors above where goods from the river were hoisted to the loft. There is history in pub-names too— *The Custom House* and the *Dublin Packet* remind us that the city was once the chief port trading with Ireland.

As we walk about we find many things to remind us today of days gone by. Many buildings are largely rebuilt 19th century travesties of the old city—but the Rows remain unique, two storeys of walk-ways, parts of which date back to the 13th century. Many shops still have vaulted crypts where mediaeval merchants stored their goods. They give a dry walkway for shoppers and are linked to a new shopping precinct hidden behind them. Chester people like to live upstairs and even Victorian houses on the outskirts are reached by a flight of steps to first floor level.

The best vantage point from which to see the city is the city wall, which charmed Dr Johnson's Boswell. Apart from a small break where the County Hall was built, it remains the most complete town wall in England. Parts near the North Gate are much as they were in the 3rd century AD when built by the Romans. It was here that the famous collection of Roman carved stones in the Grosvenor Museum was found. The Roman soldiers used stones from the cemetery outside the North Gate to repair the Walls. The Water Tower, standing at the end of a spur-wall, was once the key defence of the port of Chester until the river changed its course as a result of the Norman weir built to power the mills, which reduced the flow rate and silting made it impossible for boats to reach the city wall. The Roodee, where the Chester Races are run, was created by the river's change in course. The name derives from 'Rood Eye' — the Island of the Cross — the base of the old stone cross is still to be seen. Behind the stands we find the stonework of the old wharf where the Roman traders unloaded their vessels.

King Charles' Tower reminds us of that day in 1645 when King Charles I stood here to watch the rout of his forces on Rowton Moor. We think of the stirring times when we walk inside the tower, for here is a museum of the Civil War in Cheshire. We remember Sir Geoffrey Shakerley, whose monument is in Lower Peover Church, rowing across the river to his monarch in an old tub, and of that ill-fated rising of 1659 — just a year before the Restoration, under the leadership of Sir George Booth; a rising which incidentally started in Chester and ended with the battle of Winnington Bridge, near Northwich, the last battle of the Civil War. The towers are administered by the Grosvenor Museum which itself contains important Roman collections illustrating life in the Fortress. 'Period rooms' and various historical objects illustrate life in the city in more recent years.

The walls overlook the Dee where there are three sets of three steps known as the Wishing Steps. One is supposed to hop from top to bottom, to the top and then to the bottom again without drawing a breath in order for the wish to be fulfilled. Near the steps are the lovely tree-lined walks on the Dee side where boats may be hired, or where peaceful afternoons may be spent sitting in the sun and feeding the swans. Bands play from the Victorian bandstand, and a summer Sunday afternoon in 'The Groves' has an air of more leisurely days.

The church of St. John looks over the river above the little Hermitage on its rock where they say King Harold came after the Battle of Hastings to spend his last days. Ethelred the Saxon founded the church after a dream that he should do so at the place where he saw a white deer. The church was built again after the Norman Conquest, when a rule was introduced that the bishop had to have his cathedral in the largest town in the diocese, forcing the Bishop of Lichfield to move to Chester. Inside are the finest Norman arcades in the county with arcades in the triforium and clerestory above them, as examples of the transition from Norman to 'Early English' architecture. One of the great columns has a painting of St John the Baptist with an open book on which lies the Lamb of God. In 1975 the church held its 1,000th birthday celebrations. Its organ was used at Queen Victoria's Coronation and transported here by canals, which were at the height of their popularity at the time. A collection of crosses showing Nordic influences are housed at the west end of the church, along with old carved stones and effigies. The Tower fell down in the 19th century, and the east end was allowed to decay, when the college and chantries were closed down after the Reformation. St John's is now a shadow of its former glory, yet close by the Roman amphitheatre has been partly excavated and we may walk where the Romans once trod. We can see the entrance ways, with the remains of gates which could only be locked by those not in the arena, we can also sit in the little room where those who were to fight would wait. Here is a touching link with the Romans, a small altar set up as a result of a vision by Sextus Marcianus where prayers were offered to the Goddess Nemesis who ruled the arena.

A selection of Roman stone-work, including a reconstructed hypocaust, is on show in the 'Roman Gardens' close to the Newgate and a corner tower of the fortress has been excavated close to it, its remains being preserved for us to see. The arch we pass through is called the 'Wolf' or 'Pepper Gate'. An old Chester tale tells how the mayor's daughter eloped with her lover through the gate centuries ago. The mayor retaliated by having the gate locked permanently. An old proverb in the city is 'to lock the Pepper Gate after the daughter has been stolen .

In 'The British Heritage' reconstruction, models and a slide show tell the story of the city, and a part of the Rows in Victorian times has been reconstructed. The old Church of St Michael has been converted into a centre where the city shows visitors the way in which it conserves its ancient buildings. Chester Cathedral is a conglomeration of different styles (a textbook for students of Gothic architecture), the west door was to be flanked by twin towers but work stopped at the Reformation, leaving the buttresses without a definite function. It was Henry VIII who confiscated the Abbey of St Werburgh and created the diocese of Chester with the old 'Abbey' restyled the 'Cathedral'.

That fact has left Chester with a heritage of some of the finest monastic remains in the land, such as the monks' refectory, preserved because Henry founded the King's School in the building. Its lovely pulpit, from which a monk would read while the brothers ate, is one of the only three which survive in England.

The cloisters at Chester are a delight, with the pool in the centre where the abbey's water supply was piped in the Middle Ages — despite a dispute with the Merton family who were granted land by Edward I when he gave their home at Marton to Vale Royal Abbey. The family were perhaps rather disenchanted with monks in general and cut the pipes, but were ordered to restore them by the courts of the time. There would have been open windows in monastic days when Ranulph Higden penned his history of the world called *Polychronicon* and wrote the famous Chester plays here. Today they contain an interesting gallery of saints and their special days throughout the year. One of the oldest things in the city is the font dating from the fourth century and originally made for a church in Italy. It stands under Norman arches in a pleasing setting. The Consistory Court has a charming Jacobean setting at the south west, where a tower was planned. We climb well-worn steps to enter the court-room under a screen rich with Jacobean carvings; inside it is just as it has always been, with fine old blackened woodwork.

Modern woodwork is found in the crucifix above the chancel gates; it came from Oberammergau in the Tyrol. The gates crown Chester's glorious 14th century choir-stalls, which have many links with the Nantwich set, suggesting the same carpenters carved them. On one we find the legend of St Werburgh, who was the daughter of a king of Saxon Mercia. She is seen with the geese that were pets of an old woman and had been eaten by a robber. Only the bones were left and the old woman was heart-broken. Werburgh prayed and the geese returned from the dead. Her own bones were carried here in the 9th century from Staffordshire to save them from the Danes. We find the lovely shrine built to hold them in the 13th century in the Lady Chapel, lovingly restored and again rich with paint. This Early English chapel is one of the most beautiful parts of the old building.

The transepts at Chester are uneven, a small one to the north a large one to the south. When the monks wanted more room in the 14th century, they could not extend north as the abbey buildings were there, instead they extended south over the site of the Parish Church of St Oswald. They built a new church for the parishioners who used it for a time, but then demanded to be allowed to use the transept as their church. The structure built for them still survives and, having had many uses since the 14th century, it is now a supermarket.

Much was restored in the 19th century by Scott, who left us two pleasing comments on his time. Carved at the end of the south transept are Disraeli with a sword defending the Crown, and Gladstone overthrowing the Irish Church. One of the choirstalls is a sad reminder of days of the recent past. Placed here when the stalls were restored, it has the inscription 'League of Nations to the Rescue' — the hopes of peace after the First World War that were shattered in 1939. A rare treasure is the 'cobweb picture', a small painting of the Virgin and Child painted on a fabric woven from caterpillar silk, but always known as spider's web. It keeps company with a narwhale's tusk carved to form the shaft of a processional cross. The Cathedral Square with its Georgian houses is worth a visit, as is the small chapel of the Bishops of Chester with its rich 17th century carvings and plaster-work.

Chester has spread outside the walls and today the area within them is largely uninhabited, being the shopping and entertainment centre. Her old churches do not have parishioners living nearby and therefore some of these churches have been put to other uses. Holy Trinity is now the Guildhall and a museum of the guilds of Chester. St Peter's Church at the centre, with the old cross set up again in front of it, stands where the Roman headquarters was and continues as a place of worship. Inside it is furnished with 17th and 18th century fittings.

The great cutting for the canal is crossed by the delicate 'Bridge of Sighs' linking the site of the old prison and the chapel in the Bluecoat School where prisoners would be taken for their last prayers. The cruel prison, with its tradition of placing the executed heads above the Northgate, has long gone, but the school building founded by Bishop Stratford is still standing, with a statue of a bluecoat boy reading from a book over the doorway.

Thomas Harrison was the architect of Chester Castle. He demolished most of the mediaeval building and created one of the finest classical buildings in the land. He rebuilt the North Gate and designed the Grosvenor bridge. His elegant classical designs are a contrast to the Gothic town hall and the stark modern development next to it. When they demolished the old market hall to build the new one, we were able to examine the remains of the headquarters of the Roman Fortress, a workshop and an unusual building with an oval courtyard with fountains. Close by a bath house was traced, then all was destroyed apart from one small piece of stonework left as a reminder. Surely the most tragic and uninspiring Roman 'relic' anywhere!

The old Leeche House with its fine Tudor chimney piece (now an antique shop) has a strange wooden construction, where residents could look down on visitors while remaining unseen. There is also the lovely plaster-work of God's Providence House. An inscription saying 'God's Providence is Mine Inheritance' was set up when this was the only house to escape the plague — apparently because it had a bunch of onions hanging by the door! Tudor House, said to be the oldest in the city, is an antique shop. Gammul House is where the Mayor of Chester entertained King Charles while he made plans for the battle of Rowton and we may look round the 16th century Stanley Palace.

The Rows have excellent shops (Brown's is known as one of the foremost department stores in the world). The Gateway Theatre with its repertory company is a new building with wide views to Wales; a splendid sight at night with street-lights looking like fairy lights in the distance.

Outside the walls Chester has rows of Victorian and thirties' style houses and a few large modern concrete blocks. There are interesting warehouses along the canal and imposing hotels by the station, one with a statue of Queen Victoria. Chester is also a rail centre. Close to the station is what looks like a factory chimney until we notice windows and a lift shaft. It is, in fact, the last shot tower in England. The lift is an addition of the last decade, the rest takes us back to days before mechanisation in industry. Boiling lead was dropped from the top of the tower into a container of water at the bottom forming tiny balls, used as shot for guns.

Chester has three bridges over the Dee. A suspension bridge carries a footway high above the river while the Old Dee Bridge is a fine mediaeval bridge with its spaces over the cut-waters for pedestrians to dodge out of the way of traffic. The sandstone was quarried on the far bank of the Dee. It was said at the time that the Black Prince preferred to build the bridge in stone, rather than use timber from the forests because this would impair hunting. On the far bank we see the quarries where the sandstone for Roman Chester was obtained. There is a little shrine with a carved image of Minerva with her owl. A remarkable point is that she was given a crown in the Middle Ages and was venerated as a statue of the Madonna. There were many statues of Roman matrons in churches in mediaeval Europe venerated as Madonnas, but this is the only example in the North West. The statue is protected by iron rails, but is in need of more care and protection as weather and litter are taking their toll on the only Roman shrine preserved above ground in this country.

It was here that King Edgar had his Hall and was rowed on the Dee by seven princes who assembled to show their subjection. The panorama of the river and city from Handbridge is particularly fine. Handbridge boasts the new church of St Mary-without-the-Walls, which overlooks the old church of St Mary on the Hill. It is a pretty structure which contains some fine monumental effigies and a splendid ceiling by the same craftsmen who made the ones at Astbury and Witton. There are boats in this part of the Dee too, but these are the working boats of the salmon fishers. You can sometimes see the salmon jumping over the weir by the Old Dee Bridge. The road to Wales today crosses the Dee on the Grosvenor Bridge, built in 1832 and opened by Princess Victoria, five years before she became queen. It was the largest span stone arch in the world at the time.

Chester is a city of many delights and there is always something unusual to discover in this city by the Dee.

Around Chester

CHESTER provides a good starting point to explore much of the county. At Upton, the zoo in the grounds of a Victorian Mansion had small beginnings before the Second World War, but has grown to be one of the finest zoos in the world. It is in pleasant grounds with the animals displayed in settings which are as near to their natural habitat as possible in our climate. There are also indoor exhibits including a nocturnal house and an aquarium. Facilities for refreshments and lovely gardens make a visit to the zoo a thoroughly enjoyable day out and there is an added attraction of boat tours around the enclosures. A public garden at Upton has the remains of a cock pit where the Victoria Hotel stood, a memory of less kind days.

The main road takes us to *Tarvin*, a Welsh name indicating a border and possibly indicating some British settlement here years ago. It is lucky in that it was one of the first places to have a by-pass. Traffic coming into the village street is usually village traffic, which is fortunate for only a few hundred yards away the heavy traffic of the Manchester-North Wales road trundles by. Tarvin has a medley of buildings, some set on the living rock, and some old cottages have a platform of solid sandstone where one would expect to find a garden. There is a delightful little opening that leads to a tiny world of old cottages, flowers, and red sandstone - one of the prettiest little spots in Cheshire. There are some houses of Georgian times and a row of charming old-fashioned black and white cottages near the splendid old church with its tower looking far too large for it. This was to have been the start of a rebuilding operation in the 15th century but was doomed to remain incomplete, leaving the 14th century church looking rather diminutive in comparison.

We come to the churchyard through 18th century gates with a quaint hearse-house of the same period by their side. We remember John Bruen of Stapleford, well-known in the county for his goodly ways, so that travellers to Ireland made a point of calling to spend the night at his home before making their way through Chester to the port at Neston. They would travel on feeling the better for their stay with such a good man and from all parts of the countryside, gentlemen sent their children to hear his teaching. His house, Stapleford Hill, was demolished and replaced by an 18th century mansion, which is now a farmhouse. Old John removed all the stained glass windows of Tarvin which contained paintings of saints and other things deemed to be 'Popish idols' by the fervently anti-popish Puritans. A book of his life was published by the preacher of Bunbury, who records that John reglazed the church with clear glass at his own expense. One almost feels his hopes that this hint might have sent another John Bruen to Bunbury to do the same there.

The name John Bruen is carved on the church roof, it was perhaps his son who was warden there when it was built. One carving that escaped John's attention is the Tarvin Imp, high up on the south wall he keeps watch on the altar through a 'squint' (an opening allowing those in the side chapel to see the high altar).

When John died in 1623, even the vicar was moved to poetry and wrote in the registers:-

> *An Israelite in whom no guyle*
> *or fraud was ever found,*
> *a Phoenix rare, whose virtues fair*
> *through all our coasts do sound.*

There is a reminder of the Civil War too, Henry Hardware's brass monument of the 16th century has a hole made by a musket ball.

Not far from here, the traveller who is adventurous will find the long lane in the Parish of *Hockenhull* which leads to the three little packhorse bridges which cross the Gowy. They have splendid cobbled surfaces and are in a remarkable state of preservation. No buildings are near and the whole setting is so perfect that we would not be surprised to see a train of pack-horses coming from the salt towns and going towards Chester as they must have done so often. Old cottages and farmhouses abound in this district; there is the pretty village of Willington to explore, or the famous *Headless Woman Inn* at *Duddon,* which revives the tale of a serving maid, beheaded because she would not tell the hiding place of the Hockenhull treasure. There are some fine old halls too, *Burton Hall* in a leafy lane has a gabled front looking out to its old dove-cote, a rare survival in Cheshire. *Huxley Lower Hall* sits in a valley where the little river Gowy has been tapped to fill its moat, which it obligingly does, then flows gently on its way again. The Hall is a fine 17th century brick building with an archway and gate for us to enter by after we have crossed the bridge. It is a pleasant prospect for those who care to look at it from the hill above the river valley, mellow in its setting of meadows and trees.

Tattenhall church was mainly rebuilt last century, but it has an old tower and fine wrought iron gates. The churchyard is pleasing with old gravestones and a sundial, and we make our way to it by a small street with old half-timbered cottages. There are some splendid houses in the main street, and a fine old Jacobean Hall with high gables, standing by a pool. The secondary school has now re-opened as a centre for children to spend a few days in residential study of special topics. The pupils now go to Malpas where a new comprehensive school has been formed called the 'Heber High' after the famous son of Malpas, Bishop Heber, who became Bishop of Calcutta and wrote the well-known hymns *From Greenland's Icy Mountains* and *Holy Holy Holy.* He has a window in his memory at Malpas Church. A large new primary school, has a stone lion growling in its direction from a nearby house.

Hargrave and *Hartshill* are two interesting villages, both have little churches dating from the early years of the 17th century which are very like each other. Hartshill was built in 1609 and Hargrave in 1627 by Thomas Moulson the son of a local farmer who became lord mayor of London. He was forced to walk to school in Tarvin as a boy and one evening was returning home with his friend in pouring rain to find the river Gowy was too flooded to cross. The pair spent the night under a haystack and vowed that if they became rich, Hargrave would have its own school and church to save future children suffering as they had done; a tale worth remembering in these days, when children travel to and from school in special buses.

The attractive village of *Christleton* is noted for having won the Cheshire Best Kept Village award several times while Christleton players present some adventurous outdoor dramas. The little church, mostly rebuilt during the last century, is the focal point of the village. Christleton Hall is now a college, but was the outpost of the Royalists when Chester was besieged, and it was nearby Rowton Moor that Charles I's army was defeated.

Vicar's Cross has a golf course and ribbon development along the busy road to Manchester. One house of interest was built to look like the bridge of a boat. There are the delightfully named *Guilden Sutton, Mickle Trafford* and *Wimbolds Trafford* to explore, and places like *Cotton Edmunds* and *Cotton Abbots* whose inhabitants may be counted on your fingers. *Barrow* has an old church that has been renewed over the years. The churchyard features in an interesting tale of 1613, when it was mentioned in a case heard in Star Chamber.

The Puritan gentry of the district had travelled around destroying stone crosses, including the one in the churchyard at Barrow. The account of their reasons for destroying them gives us good documentation for the use of crosses in mediaeval times and explains why the Puritans were keen to get rid of what they believed were 'graven images'. *'Travellers would stop and worship at them, and funeral parties stopped and said prayers by them'.* While it sounds innocent to us, it was deemed to be superstitious and sinful in 17th century England.

Barrow is by the little river Gowy and we come to it by turning off the main road at *Stamford Bridge,* a name which indicated it was here the Roman road crossed the river (stone-ford). Further along the Manchester Road we come to Delamere Forest and two lovely turnpike cottages. At *Mouldsworth* there is an unusual motor museum in an old water works, with vintage cars and a reconstruction of a contemporary garage.

Plemstall Church has no village, and its only disturbance is the train which rattles past between Chester and Manchester. It is a place for pilgrims for it is one of the few places in Cheshire directly associated with a saint. Here in the days before the Gowy valley had been drained and the waters confined to their present channel, was a marshy area with a small island where Pledgemund the Hermit lived. When Alfred the Great was defending Anglo-Saxon England against the Danes he called this quiet hermit to be his archbishop and installed him at Canterbury. Pledgemund penned the *Saxon Chronicles* and was part of the inspiration behind the so-called 'Winchester School' of manuscripts. He died in 914, having crowned Edward the Elder, King of England.

The church is a storehouse of lovely things, it has a single row of columns in the Welsh tradition, box pews, a trio of candelabra and a three-decker pulpit. Much of the woodwork was carved and presented by the aptly named clergyman Reverend Toogood, who was at the church from 1907 to 1946. There is old woodwork in the roof and an imposing pew made for the churchwardens when their position was one of the most important in any community. Outside the church is a large monument to the Hurlestons with skeletons carved on it. Pledgemund's well survives too, not far from the church. It is said to have been a Druidic centre long before Pledgemund arrived and certainly sacred wells were part of the Celtic religion. When we throw a coin into a 'wishing well' we are in effect paying tribute to the Celtic spirits.

Saughall has an interesting windmill now converted into a dwelling. Its gruesome name, 'Gibbit Mill' reminds us of the practice of hanging the bodies of executed criminals in iron frames near the scene of the crime or the execution.

Saighton, to the south, takes its name from an old word for willows. Cheshire has two very rare monastic granges, which belonged to the Benedictine monks and were in reality rich country houses for the abbots and their guests, while the more common Cistercian granges were farms.

Ince has the remains of its Abbot's House still standing as a group of cottages. Here at Saighton is the magnificent gateway built in the 15th century. We catch a glimpse of it from the road and are impressed by the grandeur of the way of life of the Benedictine abbots. We tend to think of monks living very simple and frugal lives and forget that the abbots were considered to be like the nobles of the county, and as great landowners they lived in the style of noble lords. It was in splendid buildings like this that important visitors would stay. Today only the gatehouse stands with Abbot Simon Ripley's arms carved on it and a madonna in a niche. The rest was a Victorian creation of Lady Grosvenor whose husband died before coming Duke of Westminster. She remarried the promising politician George Wyndham, but the strain of trying to deal with the Irish problems proved too much for him and she was left a widow again, while her son was killed in the First World War. Her motto might well have been that carved on a Tudor beam, 'Do not give way to troubles, but go on more boldly against them'. She devoted her time to creating the lovely house and grounds of Saighton - it is a school today but a place of rare enchantment and a fragrant memory of a beautiful lady destined to a sad life.

The Wirral - God's Acre

WHEN the Cheshire prophet Robert Nixon was asked where people could escape the terrible events he prophesied, he replied 'In God's Acre—betwixt the Mersey and the Dee'.

Much of the Wirral has been given to Merseyside now, but Cheshire retains a foothold on the lands between the Mersey and the Dee. The bank of the Mersey has a romantic history, with the story of *Stanlow Abbey,* founded in 1178 and moved to Whalley in Lancashire in 1296 because of continual flooding. The great monuments here are the modern oil-refineries at Stanlow, which can be seen for miles as most major oil companies have terminals here.

Ellesmere Port is one of the busiest industrial centres in the North West. It took its name from Ellesmere in Shropshire, when the Shropshire Union Canal was constructed. Shropshire, in 1795, was the scene of much industrial activity, and it was intended that this canal should become the link with the sea for her industries. The district took its name because it was the port for Ellesmere; today it is part of the port of Manchester.

There are old warehouses by the canal where the goods were loaded and unloaded. It is still a quiet place with interesting corners and is sometimes called 'Little Venice'. There is a museum of inland navigation amongst the old warehouses and docks, with exhibits of boats and barges to remind us of days when the North West showed the world the value of canal transport. Up to 1887 the town was a bustling little place thriving on the canal trade, but in that year work started on construction of the Manchester Ship Canal. Prosperity has followed and many industries which rely upon imports have developed here. Ellesmere Port has new shops and civic buildings, banks and offices, excellent leisure facilities, new housing estates and schools, which help to make this one of the most modern towns in the county.

My favourite tale of these parts is the one of the Stanney Duck. A ghost of a duck (of all things) had been seen in a lane and the local parson tried in vain to exorcise it. The local butcher declared that he could do better and chased the bird with his axe. He succeeded in cutting off its head, but since that day the lane has been haunted by the spectacular spectre of a headless duck.

The southern coast of Wirral looks out over the Dee with its sand flats and salt marshes, the haunt of many species of sea-birds. The Welsh Mountains on the other side of the river stand out against the setting sun and give this area of the county a reputation for some of the most picturesque sunsets in the world. Here we find *Parkgate* — developed as a port for travellers from the South making their way to Dublin after the port of Chester silted up. Now the quay wall here is high and dry too, with sand and grass where boats once were moored. The 18th century was the hey-day of Parkgate and many famous people came this way. Handel composed much of the *Messiah* while he waited for his boat here in 1741. Today it is a quiet suburb where the watch house waits for ships that will not come and where the donkey stand, celebrated ice-cream and shrimps, are memories of former days before the sea deserted it.

William Grenfell was born in the same house Handel stayed in. His early adventures on this coast equipped him for a life of adventure as a doctor and missionary amongst the fisherfolk of Labrador. As 'Grenfell of Labrador' he became a real-life hero. It was from here too that William of Orange sailed on that fateful expedition which culminated in the Battle of the Boyne and made Ireland (at least nominally) Protestant, and caused orange to become the colour of Protestants in Ireland.

Close by is *Neston*—the birth-place of Emy Lyon in 1761. Her father, a blacksmith, died when she was still a girl and she and her mother carted coal in donkey panniers to help supplement her mother's earnings as a domestic servant. The girl went to London at the age of 17, to work as a nurse and she soon became known for her beauty. Her first major conquest, Charles Greville, heir to an earldom, arranged for her to learn reading, music and other social arts and graces. Romney fell under her spell and painted no less than 23 portraits of her, as did Reynolds, Lawrence and Hopner. At the age of 25 she was in Naples where she met Sir William Hamilton, Ambassador to the Court. He married her in London and returned to Naples where she became a close friend of the queen and was popular in the court. It was there she met Nelson after his victory at the battle of the Nile. They fell in love and Nelson's career was almost ruined by his scandalous association with her. He lived in the same house as the married couple when they returned to London and when he died left her £4,000. She had become used to extravagant living and this was soon spent so that she died in poverty after a time spent in prison for debt. The cottage where she was born still stands; by the standards of the time, it seems to have been quite substantial and prosperous.

Neston has fine 18th century houses and an interesting church with some Saxon carvings, relics of a church which had a priest when the Domesday Book was compiled. Most of it has been restored and repaired, so that there is little that it truly old, apart from an interesting grave slab showing a floriate cross coming from the mouth of a strange face. This adaptation of the 'Green Man' fertility figure of pre-Christian days is also seen on a grave slab at Norton Priory. The original 'Green Men' were sacrifices at spring time to make sure the crops grew, but this is a Christian adaptation; a symbol of the resurrection that is due to all Christians.

The village of *Burton* is one of the loveliest in these parts and it welcomes us to its manor today where we may spend a weekend in study at one of a host of widely different topics. It is the Adult College of the county, one of a number set up after the Second World War to enable people to spend a few days with those who share a similar interest, under expert tuition and in pleasant surroundings. It was the home of the Congreves who have the distinction of having a father and son who both gained the Victoria Cross. At the gates of the college is a cottage which sits on an outcrop of rock looking rather like a beached ship. It must have been quite new when Bishop Wilson was born there in the 17th century. His proudest boast was that he was 'the poorest bishop in Europe' and he is still remembered in histories of the Isle of Man. He served there for 58 years being buried on the island in 1755, having earned the reputation of a saint. Burton is a pretty village with rock-cut streets and an assortment of interesting houses, it is a truly old fashioned water-side place with its wide views over the sands of the Dee to the Welsh Mountains.

Burton Church is a peaceful spot, with Georgian gate-posts,

hidden away from the village street. Much rebuilt in 1721, it has a chapel of 1380 and a font looking like two drums which may be Norman. Close to the churchyard are two headstones with their inscriptions long weathered away of two Quakers whose wish it was to lie here outside the churchyard. A sad little stone was set up in recent years to the memory of Father Plessingron, who was executed in 1679. A chalice and a gibbet are carved on it in memory of an English martyr. He was hanged, drawn and quartered at Chester after Titus Oates had spoken of a Catholic plot against the Crown. His remains were taken to Puddington Hall and were to have been exhibited — one quarter on each corner of the roof — but he was well-loved by the Catholic family there and his remains were secretly given Christian burial here. The last of the old family of Massey of Puddington is also buried here without a memorial. He joined the Old Pretender in the 1714 rebellion, and after the defeat at Preston, he rode back to Puddington, non-stop, swimming the Mersey en route. His horse dropped dead at the gate and the sixty-year old Jacobite retired to bed — he was arrested and taken to Chester castle where he died shortly after.

Willaston in Wirral — is a place of beauty with a fine old three-gabled stone Hall of 1558 and a 17th century inn in the middle of the peninsula. The Nordic lands to the west have been given up now, but Thurstaston Common where Thor's stone is, and the Thingwall where the Norsemen met for their parliament, are worth mentioning.

Backford is a pleasing spot on the road from Chester to the Wirral. It has a little mediaeval church rich with paintings by Edward Frampton, including the creator sitting on a rainbow above the chancel arch. It has a churchyard noted for interesting gravestones, produced by a local stone-mason at the end of the 18th and start of the 19th centuries who felt he had poetic talents. An example, set up to Samuel Lewis who died aged just 19, is typical:

> *Sing and Pray without delay,*
> *You do not know the time;*
> *For I was one that soon was gone,*
> *And cut off in my prime.*

The church possesses some rare painted coats-of-arms by the last of the Randle Holmes of Chester. He quarrelled with the College of Heralds who ordered that his work should be removed from all churches, but this group escaped their notice. Backford Hall is a lovely house with wooded gardens, a splendid old tree guarding the entrance and coats-of-arms on the walls. Here George Ormerod penned his history of Cheshire and George Birkenhead the poet also lived here.

Wirral main roads are rather dull, running direct to the main towns, but there are byways that can be explored by the motorist or cyclist and it is the happy discovery of some unexpected place, or an unexpected panorama when one turns a corner that makes Cheshire such a delight to explore. If we turn off near the Atomic Energy Authority plant at *Capenhurst*, for example, we can find ourselves looking round the village of *Shotwick*. The place was once of great importance, standing on the very edge of the Dee, though today some two miles of land separate it from the water — as a result of drainings and siltings. Its old church stands like a fortress guarding what used to be the main road into Wales. There was a ford here and Henry III and Edward I used the castle in their wars with Wales. We come to Shotwick via a long winding lane which follows a brook for much of its route. Close to the church the remains of the mediaeval roadway over the Dee to Flint may be traced, an old bridge crossing the brook as it flows to join the Dee. It was known as 'the Saltesway' — one of the old trade routes which took salt from Cheshire into Wales. The spot still reminds us of those days long ago, when this tall church tower acted as a look-out and fortress in times of trouble, and as a landmark for boats which would tie up at the creek formed by the brook. The old Hall was fortified too, but only the moat now remains.

The church is pleasing, with a single row of columns in the Welsh tradition, and a three decker pulpit typical of the 18th century. There are old box pews with doors to keep out draughts and a gravestone with ICC carved on it — said to be the bit and stirrups of Squire Hockenhull who died when his horse stepped into a rabbit hole while he was hunting. In truth they stand for 'John Carter Curate' and date from the 16th century when 'I' and 'J' were both represented by the same letter.

In this parish lived Mary Davies in the 17th century. She survived her husband by more than 30 years and it was as an old woman, who had served as the parish midwife for many years, that she first showed signs of horns, which were to grow time and again to earn her a place amongst England's curiosities. It is recorded that one of them — some 9 inches long and 2 inches thick was given as a present to the King of France. They were shed at intervals and some found their way to the British and Ashmolean Museums.

In *Thornton Le Moors*, Elton Hall of the 17th century keeps company with the large cooling towers of the 20th. The little mediaeval church has some old furnishings and panels round the sanctuary made of old box pews. Nearby are pleasant old houses and in green fields not too far away are the ruins of the little chapel of *Wervin*, formerly belonging to the Abbot of Chester.

It is an area of great change, but the view over the Dee with the Welsh mountains will endear itself to all. Each spring and autumn crowds gather to see the spectacle of the Dee Bore. Though not as spectacular as the Severn Bore, it is still worth the wait to see the tidal wave, followed by smaller ones come up the river like some great animal travelling just under the surface. It must have impressed the Romans when they were at Chester, and stirred the Celts who gave this river its name — that of the water goddess. It is a kindly river, said to give up all who are drowned in it with a light mysteriously shining over the place where the body may be found. The Mersey on the other hand is said to take a human life as a sacrifice every five years. Anyone who falls into the Mersey today is given immediate medical treatment in case of pollutant poisoning!

The Dee saw much of our early history and gave us well-loved poems. Charles Kingsley wrote of the maid who, when bringing her cattle home over the sands of Dee, drowned after getting lost in mist as the tide came in

> *And never home came she*
> *But still the boatmen hear her call the*
> *cattle home*
> *Across the sands of Dee.*

John Milton penned his *Lycidas* after his friend John King had died when his ship had floundered and sunk in calm weather within a few miles of Parkgate. And in far lighter vein, there was also 'the Jolly Miller who lived by the Dee'.

The Mersey has seen the industrial growth of the 19th and 20th centuries: its history is still in the making. It is believed the Mersey channel was blocked in early times — perhaps as late as the Roman occupation for the Romans had no name for the estuary. The clearing of the postulated sand-bank occurred in time for the Mersey to take over when Chester's port declined because of the silt and Liverpool developed as a port as the 'brainchild' of King John.

The Welsh Border

> *Taffy was a Welsh man Taffy was a thief,*
> *Taffy came to our house and stole a piece of beef,*
> *I went to Taffy's house, Taffy was not home,*
> *Taffy came to our house and stole th'mutton bone.*
> *I went to Taffy's house, Taffy was in bed,*
> *So I upped with the chamber pot and threw it at his yed.*

The boundaries with Wales were always troubled and it was not until the Tudor period that they were fixed on the river Dee. King Offa built his Dyke to keep the Welsh at bay, the Normans built a line of Motte and Bailey castles and Edward I pushed into Wales from Chester much as Suetonius Paulinus had marched into Anglesey ten centuries before.

Now all is peaceful in the Dee valley, but there are memories of more turbulent days when the Welsh came this way on their cattle raids and 'stole a piece of beef'. At *Malpas,* in the county's south western corner, a mound by the church is a reminder that a Norman castle once stood there and that this was the seat of one of the powerful barons who helped Hugh Lupus keep control of the border-lands. Malpas is a lovely old town though its name suggests it was a bad (mal in French) pass into Wales. It stands on a hill with old houses, one by the church has a row of columns looking strangely Roman. There are other attractive old buildings, including an inn with a chair in which James I sat.

This old village is crowned by one of the finest old churches in the county, looking like a fortress from outside. It may have had its origins in a tiny monastery for two Cluniac monks belonging to the Priory at Mantacute in Somerset. This could be the root of the tradition of having two incumbents in the church which continued until the 19th century. The gates are attractive in wrought iron and an old chest of the 13th century is also rich with wrought iron, said to be by the same craftsmen who made the famous cope-chest in Chester Cathedral. The interior is light and graceful, with two very interesting altar tombs. The Brereton Chapel contains the tomb of Sir Randle and Lady Brereton of 1522 — one of the high spots of mediaeval art in Cheshire. The Knight is a Galahad in armour, the lady has angels to support her pillow and lap dogs bite at the folds of her dress. They are a lovely couple of the time of Henry VII. Around the tomb stand figures of their children. It was Randle's son who was executed by Henry VIII on a charge of adultery with Anne Boleyn. Hugh and Lady Cholmondeley are a dapper pair of Elizabethans and while there is only 70 years between these two monuments, they are worlds apart in style and feeling, coming from two very different ages. In between the two burials, the Reformation had taken place and there was the new Tudor Protestant prosperity. The difference between the simple faith of the Brereton monument and the ostentatious show of the Cholmondeley monument is striking. The simple gown of Lady Brereton and the sumptuous farthingale of Lady Cholmondeley are in complete contrast. On the Cholmondeley tomb are a babe in swaddling clothes with their son Hugh and Lady Mary Cholmondeley, the most ambitious Cheshire woman of her age, mentioned elsewhere for her law-suits and purchase of Vale Royal. Mary married Hugh, Cheshire's first member of Parliament at Westminster, and took charge of raising the Cheshire troops for the defence against the Armada.

The chapel has some fine old glass imported from the Continent and a charming group of old coffin plates placed here when the vaults were repaired. The screens around the two chapels are particularly fine. Some of the tracery heads were damaged and were restored with iron castings from those that remained in the last century. The church had choir stalls, from the same hands as the Chester and Nantwich set but only three remain. The roof is rich with carvings and there are hatchments and the Royal Arms hanging above the Nave. Around the pulpit are mediaeval encaustic tiles and the vestry is said to be from designs by Vanbrugh.

A sad story is told in the registers of 1625. Richard Dawson of

Bradley, knowing he was soon to die of the plague and that he was too heavy for his nephew and a servant girl to bury, who were all that remained from a household of nine, dug his own grave, put straw at the bottom, covered himself up with warm clothes and lay down to die.

Shocklach is so little — some maps do not even show it! At the end of a lane is a tiny church; if it ever had a village, it has long since been deserted. There are two mounds where a castle stood shortly after the Conquest and much of the church is of the same date. It has a splendid Norman door and is so small that it looks as if it could not hold a congregation. The chancel was added in the 14th century to give more room, while the ceiling is a 17th century feature. Shocklach church has a bell-turret with chains hanging outside. A local tale of bells ringing at midnight is sometimes told. The reason was not supernatural, but occurred because a local joker had tied hay to the chains to attract cows. However, once a year the ghosts of the Breretons assemble in the churchyard here, riding in carriages along the country lanes to their reunion party!

Bruera too has a church little altered since the 12th century. The word Bruera means heath and the church is sometimes called Churton Heath (church on the heath). It stands in a circle of old yew trees which may have had some significance before the church was founded. It has walls some four feet thick and some fine round-headed Norman arches.

Farndon keeps watch over the Dee and over the old Dee Bridge of the 14th century. It sits on a rocky outcrop. Holt is on the other bank and a Cheshire saying is 'Go to Holt to see Farne Races' meaning to take an unnecessary length of time to say something. The bridge of nine arches dates from the middle of the 14th century with recesses above its cutwater buttresses where pedestrians could dodge out of the way of passing carts. Farndon has half-timbered houses and an old church looking over the trees towards Wales. It was garrisoned during the Civil War when Holt Castle was besieged and has one of the most interesting reminders of those days, a painted glass window showing the Royalists of Cheshire. In the centre is Francis Gammul who entertained the king in his house at Chester. The glass also shows pikemen and musketeers, a standard bearer, drummer and piper all ready to march out to fight for a lost cause. A famous son of Farndon was John Speed who produced the finest set of Elizabethan county maps, and a roadside monument recalls Roger Barnston who is remembered for his part in the Crimean War when he led the successful campaign to relieve Lucknow.

Dodleston has a church, mainly rebuilt last century, standing on the site of a chapel that was attached to a castle. Traces of the castle can still be picked out and traces of a moat are to be seen around the old rectory, on the site of the manor house. Again this was a defensive place against the Welsh after the Conquest, now it is a peaceful village. It last knew turmoil when Sir William Brereton made the village his headquarters during the siege of Chester. It has a memorial to Sir Thomas Egerton, the illegitimate son of Sir Richard Egerton of Ridley by a yeoman's daughter who became the Chancellor of England, a favourite of Elizabeth I and was made Baron Elesmere and Viscount Brackley. The Dukes of Bridgewater and the Egertons of Tatton were his descendants.

Eccleston is the Duke of Westminster's village and though stately Eaton Hall — one of the most sumptuous palaces of all time — has been demolished as an obsolete remnant of Victorian England, the new hall in ultra-modern concrete is a marvel in itself. It stands in lovely grounds with the old stable wing and a large collection of carriages still preserved. The Grosvenors own a large part of what is now central London because in 1676 Mary Davies the eleven year old heiress to what was then an insignificant estate near the capital, married Thomas Grosvenor in St. Clement Danes. They had an interesting history before that, an inn in London had the Grosvenor arms for its sign, which was seen by Lord Scrope, who had the same coat. This resulted in a court case. Both sides had good witnesses, but the majority of the Cheshire gentry who travelled to Warrington Friary to give support to the Grosvenor side were no match for the eloquence of Geoffrey Chaucer (the poet) and the famous 'Bend Or' coat was granted to the Scropes. The Grosvenors adopted the wheat-sheafs, and it is their coat, a copy of the three wheatsheaf coat of Randle de Blundville, the greatest Norman Earl, which forms the base of the county coat-of-arms.

Eccleston is a lovely village by the Dee (often visited by river-boats from Chester), with a church built by the first duke. It was to become his mausoleum, for it was completed the year that he died and inside is his magnificent effigy wearing garter robes. His son who was killed at Ypres in 1914, is shown in bronze wearing his uniform and standing by his horse.

At *Aldford* is a lovely iron bridge of 1824 designed by Thomas Telford. The village itself has houses by Douglas built for estate tenants of the Grosvenors and the remains of a Norman castle. In Stretton the old 17th century mill of the Carden estate has been restored ready to be opened to the public. *Carden* Hall burned down some years ago and the site is covered with modern country housing.

Aldersey and *Coddington* are typical old fashioned villages. A mound in Coddington is believed to be a Saxon burial mound. Perhaps a chieftain called Codda founded the village in pagan Saxon days and was buried in the centre. At *Broxton* the fine old 17th century Hall is an hotel serving first class meals in a setting of oak beams. The village is also known to locals as 'Brown Knowl' and is a pleasant little place with its post office and shops. It is the sort of traditional country village fast vanishing in these days of easy commuting. We are fortunate that the Welsh border-lands are far enough from the conurbations to be almost immune to commuters but there is a real danger of the area becoming a retirement and a weekend cottage district.

The East Cheshire plain merges into the highlands of Central

Cheshire's sandstone ridge and there are many villages with the suffix 'ley' indicating that they were clearings in woodland in Saxon times. Most of them take advantage of the natural springs that would have bubbled forth where the sandstone of the ridge meets the clay of the plain, *Faddiley*, and *Bulkley* with its lovely half-timbered post office are examples. The oddly named *Burwardsley* (pronounced Boosly) is said to have been the home of a bear-ward in the days of bear-baiting, though it is more likely that Burward was the name of the leader of the Saxon family who cleared the woodland to set up home. The *Pheasant* public house offers refreshments in a romantic setting and at evening time it is a pleasure to watch the sunset over the plain and the Welsh hills from this elevated position.

This is castle country, there is the prospect of Beeston and Peckforton castles on their hills, while *Bolesworth* and Cholmondeley (pronounced Chumley) castles are private residences of 18th/19th century construction. Cholmondeley has a lovely little private chapel with most of its 18th century fittings intact and at *Woodhey*, out in the fields, is another private chapel. Woodhey is unique in the county for it has no holy table, merely a pulpit in the centre. It is approached through a lovely 17th century loggia. The old hall it served is now gone, and nothing more than a farmhouse keeps it company. In the private pew there is a cane-work screen so that the Wilbraham's servants could sit inside keeping a watch on all that took place without being seen. It reminds me of the verse of 'All things bright and beautiful'

The rich man in his Castle, The Poor man at his gate,
He gave one lowley station, He gave one high estate.

Tushinghan-cum-grindley has a 19th century church and an old half-timbered inn. The door is dated 1667 and is new compared to the great central chimney. One of the oldest chimneys in the county, it is simply a wide open hood for the great ingle hearth, truly mediaeval in tradition. A duck once hatched from an egg here and lived in a basket by the fire. He grew up to be a bossy bird, pecking at the customers' heels until the landlord killed him. They could not eat their pet and so he was buried. His ghost returned and while a bad-tempered duck did not help trade, a ghostly one definitely reduced it! A dozen parsons assembled to charm the bird until it was small enouth to pop inside a bottle. The bottle—firmly corked—is still in the cellar wall.

Dedicated to St. Chad an old chapel is said to be on a site where he once preached. It stands out in the middle of Cheshire's green meadows at the end of a narrow lane. The brick structure was built in 1689 and still contains its old oak pews and the royal arms of George III, a reminder of the days when it was important to show your loyalty to the king as head of the Church of England as well as head of state. White owls, they say, fly from the church tower to tell a parishioner when he is to die. A Victorian hearse was recently restored and is on show in its hearse-house in the churchyard. At the picturesque *Grindley* Locks is a canal side settlement of great charm with an attractive round lock keeper's house and other Regency buildings, but remember the law still says you will be deported for seven years if you damage the canal property.

At *Overton* is an old farm, formerly the Hall, which takes us by surprise, hidden away in a hollow. It was the perfect place for the secret meetings that took place here during the Civil war. Today it is a place of peace and tranquillity with an Elizabethan half-timbered wing and gardens with pools and flowers; incidentally, it is one of the few places where farm-house Cheshire cheese is made today.

More civil war memories are to be traced at *Handley*, where the largely rebuilt church has its old tower and a roof dated 1661. It was during the siege of Chester when the Puritans had taken up position at Tattenhall, that they came this way, looking for provisions. The villagers being suspicious took refuge in the tower, whereupon the Roundheads set fire to the church in order to smoke them out.

In the hills hereabouts we find a series of wooden markers with black footprints marked with a yellow 'S'. These point the way along the 'Sandstone Trail' and lead the traveller into some of the most interesting and historic parts of the county. The path can be followed to the Bickerton Hills crowned with the remains of *Maiden Castle*, an Iron Age hill fort, on a wild hill-top. Defended on one side by a sharp cliff and on the other by a stone-faced rampart, it was found to have links with the 'timber-laced' fort walls of France. It was probably destroyed by the Romans at the time Eddisbury hill fort was demolished.

Other interesting features of these gorse covered hills are the remains of mines at *Bickerton*, where there is a tall stone chimney over the pumping engine of a long disused mine. There are disused quarries to explore and the Dropping Stone to investigate near Rawhead. See if you can spot it move — reputedly it is inching along to its destined fall. There is a shelter on Brown Knowl made out of giant slabs of stone where a hermit once lived and in 'Bloody Bones Cave' on Rawhead lived brigands who terrorised the district in the early 19th century. There is a cave known as 'the Queen's Parlour', a mine for the white sand used as scouring powder and to spread on floors in the same way that butchers spread sawdust to catch droppings. It looks as though it may have been a home for early man before that and part of the trail follows prehistoric trackways over the hills. The trail takes us through charming villages with distant prospects over the plain, there are green lanes — former important highways — to explore and a wealth of animal and plant life.

Under Beeston Cliff

For where ever a man might cast his gaze
thereabouts in the end it must return to the old grey
monarch with a castle for his crown   Beatrice Tunstall

THE ancient castle of Beeston stands a ruin today. Cromwell ordered its destruction after its part in the Civil War so that it might not be garrisoned again. The hill-top is a pleasant place for picnics and it is worth the climb today for the wide views into England and Wales.

It was these wide views that decided Earl Randle to build here in 1220. At that time the earl stood between Llewellyn the Great and Henry III, it was the time of the Welsh wars and the earl knew only too well how to play at the game of politics. When built, the castle was unlike any that had been seen in England before, being based on those that the earl had seen in the Holy Land; it has an inordinately large outer bailey, where a marching army might camp. No one could be sure which way the earl intended to use the castle. Was he intending to allow the king to use it for an offensive against Wales, or was he intending to make a pact with the Welsh and turn against his former ward and march on England? The earl died in 1237, but even then the king could not rest easy, the next earl was John le Scot, Randle's nephew but the son-in-law of Llewellyn.

William the Conqueror created his nephew Hugh Lupus the Earl of Chester and gave him all the powers of a monarch in this Palatine county. That was fine for keeping the Welsh at bay in the 11th century, but in the 13th there seemed to be too much power in Chester. Earl John was hunting with his Welsh wife at the hunting lodge in the forest at Darnhall when he was taken ill and died. It was rumoured that the Countess had poisoned him, but if Helen had any ideas of becoming dowager Countess in Chester, they were to come to nothing. Henry appointed his own son Edward, later Edward I, to be Earl in Chester as there was no male to succeed. It was this Edward who later founded Vale Royal Abbey in Cheshire and conquered Wales, making his own son Edward of Caernarvon the Prince of Wales. His building of Vale Royal and the Welsh castles was the greatest single building project in all mediaeval Europe.

Richard II, the sad monarch of Shakespeare's play, came here. He loved Cheshire and the Cheshire men, made the county a principality and they say that he hid his treasure in the well here before he left for Ireland and was captured and forced to abdicate. There have been many searches in the well which goes down some 300 ft through solid sandstone. An expedition of 1936 retrieved 25/- in copper thrown in

25

by wishmakers, but no sign of Richard's treasure was traced by them nor by a highly scientific expedition of 1976.

The castle has no true 'keep', the inner ward has round towers which were able to withstand undermining, and there are arrow-slits above the great rock-cut ditch which served as a quarry. Remains of the portcullis and draw-bridge may be traced, and there is evidence of the holes knocked through the walls for Civil War cannons. The Department of the Environment, who care for the building, have carried out extensive excavations and repairs, but are open to public criticism for building a concrete bridge over the remains of the draw-bridge — why a wooden bridge, far more in keeping with the setting and easier for future investigators to remove, if needs be, was not erected is a mystery. By the outer gate a square tower used as a latrine is a later addition. The seating was in the windows, the drain from the upper one is above the drain for the lower one — leaving visitors today to puzzle out the way in which those using the lower one ensured that no one used the one above their heads!

Visitors to Beeston today see the romantic prospect of *Peckforton* Castle rising from the trees and bracken. Built by Lord Tolmarche in the 19th century to designs by Salvin it is still a private residence. One of the high-spots of the Gothic Revival, it has been used as the backcloth for several films set in mediaeval times because original castles are usually ruins like Beeston or have been so added to in later years that they do not show a completely mediaeval face. A perfect reconstruction of a mediaeval stronghold in itself, there can be few more romantic prospects than these twin castles on their lofty hills, one the product of the troubled times of the Welsh Wars, the other of the self confidence of Victorian England.

The villages of Beeston and Peckforton are of great charm, with half-timbered cottages. A stone elephant and castle at Peckforton was made by one of the castle masons as a bee-hive, it has glass in its tiny windows. At Beeston the market is a rural affair with a beast market and household goods on sale. The canal here passes through the famous iron lock, cut through running sand, it was given its iron sides as protection. *The Wild Boar Hotel* has a first class reputation for good food, it is a fanciful half-timbered place with some older woodwork than its facade would have us believe. At Tiverton the *Crown* attracts 'real ale' drinkers, for the beer comes up from the cellars in jugs, not pumps. It too has some early half-timber work inside an 18th century structure which was once a corn exchange.

Bunbury church and village are one of Cheshire's show-pieces. Bunbury is the Clock Abbot of Beatrice Tunstall's *The Shiny Night* and by the side of the Whitchurch Road we find the 'Image House' which was the inspiration for the novel. The tale tells of a poacher who returned from his deportation to Australia and claimed the ancient right of claiming common land by having a chimney built and smoking between sunset and sunrise. He carved the squire, the sheriff and his men in sandstone and cursed them, they are all said to have died before the poacher met his maker. They are still on the walls, along with the devil, who he hoped would take their souls. Two heads capping the wooden pillars to the porch are unlike the others, more like the Celtic stone heads of the Iron Age and I can't help wondering if this is what they are — perhaps they were found after the house was built and were taken there as an apt home. The old mill at Bunbury was restored by the water authority when they built a new sewerage works next to it. Today visitors may look round and see the mill lovingly restored to working order.

There are other old buildings in the district, including the Chancery House of the 15th century where the priests to the church lived. A group of old buildings stood around the green before the war, but were destroyed by the same landmine that shook the church. It was skilfully restored by Canon Ridgway, the incumbent here at the time and one of Cheshire's antiquaries. The church is dedicated to St. Boniface, who was a missionary in Germany. We see him on a banner by the altar with the tree of Odin which he cut down, it is possible that the church was founded where news of his martyrdom first reached the king for it is his only old church in the North of England.

In the 14th century, at the same time that the Black Prince was building chapels at Vale Royal to make up for his sins in battle, his friend Hugh Calvely founded a college of canons here to pray for his soul. He rebuilt much of the church and his tomb still stands in the centre of the chancel. He was said to fight and eat like ten men and was almost 7 ft. tall, the effigy looks very like the Black Prince's. The iron hearse, with spikes to hold candles to burn for his soul is still around the tomb. The name College lane recalls the home of the canons of Hugh's church.

Brightly painted — as would have been all such tombs when new — is old George Beeston. Born in the last year of the 15th century, he died in the first year of the 17th. A friend of Drake and Raleigh, he commanded the *Dreadnought* against the Armada when he was 89 and earned a knighthood for it. Exquisitely delicate are the gates of the chapel that was built by Ralph Egerton of Ridley; carved from solid wood they have panels looking like woven twigs and the initials of husband and wife. The screens are painted with the earliest Renaissance work in the county. A brass to Ralph Egerton, the standard bearer of Henry VIII, was destroyed but a replacement, based on the drawing that Randle Holmes (one of the Cheshire heralds) prepared in the 17th century, has been set up.

There are carvings of knights and ladies in the south aisle, which form an interesting museum. They are carved from local sandstone and keep company with old carved stones, the works of the old church clock and painted saints. They were parts of old screens removed from the church years ago and rescued from store earlier in this century. Most of them are now in the care of the Victoria and Albert Museum, but it is hoped that they will be restored to the church one day. The delicate carving of the rood screen was designed by F. H. Crossley the Cheshire architect and antiquary and survived the bombing. Most of the Victorian stained glass was destroyed and the church was mainly reglazed in clear glass. Some postwar stained glass in clear bright colours has been introduced to add warmth and a gem-like quality to the windows. There are gold and blue hangings that were used in Westminster Abbey for the coronation of Elizabeth II and there is also a font of the Restoration period with a sliding cover incorporating a reading desk.

The first Methodists in Cheshire met in the vestry here which has old glass panels from Marple Hall, the birthplace of John Bradshaw who sentenced Charles I to death. Methodists at first had no intention of forming their own church. They were members of the Church of England who met together to talk about Christian things and lived their life to a strict Christian 'method'. John Wesley preached to the early fellowship under a pear tree at the moat farm in *Alpraham*.

Close to the font Jane Johnson stands in disgrace. Once placed next to the Holy table, her low cut dress was the height of fashion in her day, but did not meet with the approval of a Victorian vicar who felt that it caused improper ideas in the choir-boys. He had her removed and buried in the church-yard. When a later incumbent found her, he was convinced that she was an early statue of the Virgin, an ironic twist of fate.

Dabberland

(Dabber — an inhabitant of Nantwich)

CREWE is not really the sort of place that we would think of for a sight-seeing trip, but it has much of interest for those who study economic and social history. Crewe was created in the wake of the railways after 1837, when the first line from London to Glasgow was built. Although we would expect Crewe station to be in the centre of town, it is on the very edge as Lord Crewe did not want his estate to be affected by the railway town. The charming village of Crewe Green, with the great Jacobean Hall on one side is still delightfully rural; the town developed on the other side of the track.

The railway company gave Crewe its being, and gave the town most of its amenities. The church, the park and so on were all its products. The rows of terraced houses are not without interest, since they are neither shabby nor second rate. The men who came to work in Crewe's railway yards were skilled craftsmen and the houses that were built for them reflect this. A lovely feature of many of them is a porch with Victorian tiles half way up the walls, often showing interesting scenes on a centre panel. They came from Stoke, just over the border in Staffordshire, and are a feature of Crewe which deserves better recognition. Crewe has a fine Edwardian theatre which still produces a full programme each year. In some places the streets still retain their old fashioned stone setts.

Crewe has many amenities, an impressive library, and one of the finest modern hospitals in the land at *Leighton* nearby. A small island from the past is the largely rebuilt church and an old inn; all that remains of the old village of *Church Coppenhall* that was here before the railway came. Crewe today is a shopping centre for South Cheshire and is still a centre of production even though the days of steam trains have passed. It gives the world today the finest motor-car that money can buy, the Rolls Royce.

Nantwich is a gem. Set in the midst of some of the world's finest dairy country; its name is given to that rarest of Cheshire Cheeses — Nantwich blue fade. As long ago as the Saxon period salt was made here, and the town was second only to Chester in importance. The salt industry lapsed when production moved nearer to the main transport systems. There was some growth in the leather industry locally because of the proximity of salt and the herds of cows but Nantwich escaped developing into an industrial town. It survives today as a quaint old market town with a winding medieval street plan and lovely old houses of many periods. On one we read:-

> God grant our Ryal Queen
> In England long to reign
> For she hath put her helping hand
> To build this town again.

In 1583 the town was largely destroyed by a great fire which spread quickly through the thatched roofs of the timber houses. Bears kept behind the *Crown Hotel* were let loose and it is recorded that they ran about the streets making the women too afraid to help with fire fighting. The four bears belonging to Mr. Sackerton were mentioned in Shakespeare's *The Merry Wives of Windsor*. It must have been both alarming and distressing and the bears must have added to the general confusion. 'Praised be the Lord' wrote the parish clerk for only the day before cartloads of ammunition had been moved out of the town to Chester. The place was destitute. Elizabeth gave £2,000 along with timber from Delamere Forest towards its restoration.

The town was rebuilt and we find in its streets today some of the finest Elizabethan houses in our land. The carpenter was Thomas Clease and we can discover his name, with different spellings, on several old buildings. The elegant house he built for Richard and Margery Church, before the fire, survived. It was painstakingly restored in the years between the two wars and we may now explore the rooms upstairs, fitted out with old furnishings and curios like Nelson's sea chest. The ground floor, rich with panels, is a restaurant and we may dine by candlelight, as they did in days gone by.

Nantwich's famous hostelry is *The Crown* with an archway into which the London to Holyhead coach would drive. An interesting feature is a coach set between the bar and the dining room, with a telephone on the wall; a most unusual call box. The inn itself is one of the finest old coaching inns of England with a long gallery still used as a ballroom.

The Cheshire Cat is a night-club in what used to be alms houses. It has a mounting block outside and rich old timbering inside. Two sets of alms houses have been renewed recently and provide a fine set of old people's residences. The 17th century buildings were moved to a site beside some created by Lord Crewe in the 18th century from the former 'House of Correction'. Now they have 20th century fittings and are charming spots for senior citizens to spend the autumn years of their life.

Sweetbriar Hall is half-timbered and was saved from destruction by an architect who now has his offices there. Rotten timbers were replaced by good quality seasoned wood in the form of old railway sleepers from Crewe.

Nantwich has a 17th century bridge over the Weaver and a fine 18th century terrace by the church, which has aptly been called 'the cathedral of South Cheshire'. It never was a cathedral, in fact up to the Reformation it was only a chapel of ease to the older church at Acton. Lofty and as dignified as many a cathedral it is one of the county's treasures. Built in the 14th century, when Nantwich was proud and prosperous, it has unusual features like its octagonal central tower which make one suspect that the master masons who worked at Vale Royal, not too far away, might have had a hand in this church too. The building is in the form of a cross, and in the roof of the north transept are springers for a vault that was never added. It is said the church was left unfinished because the plague hit the town and the workmen fled. The church was completed after the plague years, but was given a less costly timber roof.

A tale about the workmen is that they made a collection each day in a pot and gave it to an old woman who purchased ale and food at a local inn for their lunch. Sure that they were not receiving their money's worth, they each agreed on the sum they would pay and then asked the landlord what he had received. Their figures did not agree, and the old woman lost her job. She found immortality, however, as the workmen carved her image in both stone and wood, being carried off by the Devil her hand still in the pot.

The glory of Nantwich is the chancel, with its old stone pulpit and its richly vaulted roof with carved bosses showing scenes from the life of the Virgin. The altar table is Tudor with carved oak legs and there is rich carving in the choir stalls, twenty in all, reputed to be the finest in the land. They are said to have come from Vale Royal, but it is more likely they were made for this place. On the tip-up seats called 'misericords' we find many carvings including some of Wyverns; 'Wyver' was an old way of pronouncing the river name Weaver and the strange beast with two legs and two wings on a dragon's body has always been associated with the river. There are many strange scenes under the seats, including wrestlers, a mermaid (a symbol of vanity, combing her hair with a glass in her hand) and the old woman with the Devil again. There is a scene of a man and his wife in a domestic fight, a pig running off with a chicken on a spit while a dog has his head in a cooking pot. We find foxes dressed as monks going to hunt and a fox pretending to be dead so that the birds come to see, whereupon he will grab the nearest one for dinner. There is also a hunting scene with a virgin in the wood. The unicorn, it is said, will lay his head in the lap of a virgin. We see them here, and a hunter about to spring out and kill him for his magic horn. What happened to the virgin then is not recorded!

An effigy in the south transept, believed to be David Craddock, has been severely damaged, partly, it is said, because the alabaster was used as a 'cure' for sheep illnesses and partly because he was torn from his tomb many years ago. He was placed on this tomb in the 1930s by F. H. Crossley, the Cheshire historian and architect. In the Civil War the church was used as a prison and Nantwich fell upon troubled times. Royalists and Roundheads battled for possession and the Royalists fired red-hot shot on the town from nearby Dorfold Hall. If the women had not carried water (there were not bears this time), the town would have been destroyed by fire again.

Dorfold Hall is one of Cheshire's finest old houses. Dated 1616, it stands at the end of a long drive and is a lovely example of the symmetrical brick buildings that were then the height of fashion. The chamber upstairs with its rich pendant plaster ceiling has been described as one of the finest in England. A room prepared for a visit by James I, who never came, has his coat-of-arms in plaster work above the mantelpiece, and the oak panels with a secret cupboard where personal things could be kept out of sight, are still there.

The house is said to stand on the site of a hunting lodge and deer-fold used by Leofric, Earl of Mercia and his wife, Lady Godiva. In the grounds is an ancient tree, reputed to mark the southern point of the old forest of Delamere.

The memory of that shrunken forest is kept alive in the name of *Acton* 'the settlement in the oaks'. The church tower here looks strangely large, and is the oldest in Cheshire. Much of the east end was made new after the Civil War and is capped with a lovely design of hearts. Inside we find two of the Wilbrahams who lived at Dorfold in the Civil War. William is a smiling cavalier with curling hair falling to his shoulders, his richly dressed wife lies by his side. They built the alms houses by the churchyard and this marble monument was set up to their memory shortly after Charles II came to the throne. A Norman font and carved stones have survived from the church that was mentioned in the Domesday Book.

When he died in 1399 William Mainwaring left his 'picture in alabaster' to cover his tomb in Acton church. It still lies in the church to which he also left a fragment of 'the true cross'. His head rests on his helmet with the donkey's head of the Mainwarings as its crest. His feet are on a lion and there are remains of paintings of the priests of Acton and surrounding churches who prayed for his soul. In the churchyard is a tall sundial, probably converted from an old cross. There is a marble gravestone too, in memory of Albert Hornby the L.C.C. cricketer, with wickets, bat and bails and a copy of his autograph.

Audlem is close to the Shropshire border, a fine old church standing on a hill which has half-round steps leading to the porch and overlooks the roof of the small market hall by the gate. When ivy was cleared from the walls, an interesting sundial scratched on a stone in one of the buttresses was found. The stone is believed to be older than the church and a relic of the early days of Christianity in the district. Most of the church is 15th century, but the chancel is older. The monks of St. Thomas' Priory in Stafford were responsible for its upkeep and refused to renew the chancel when the parishioners renewed the nave.

Moss Hall, a splendid Elizabethan half-timbered mansion in the shape of a letter 'E', has been little altered. The area also has long associations with the canals and fifteen locks carry the water over the border to Shropshire. A canal side inn here, the *Shroppie Fly*, has a barge of that name serving as its bar.

Wybunbury village is slowly sinking as natural water seepage dissolves the beds of rock salt under it. The leaning tower of Wybunbury is proverbial and has statues of saints in niches. The church has two old monuments which, hopefully, will survive when the current rebuilding on a new safer site is completed. One is the flamboyant tomb of Sir Francis and Lady Smith of Elizabeth's time, the other, a brass memorial to Ralph and Katherine Delves of Henry VII's day. Ralph was a member of an old local family whose home, *Doddington Hall*, is now a girls' school. The hall has an ancient tower in the grounds, with a Jacobean stairway and carvings which represent the four Cheshire Squires who distinguished themselves at Poitiers. They are dressed in 17th century armour as the local carver was no historian!

A long lane leads to *Baddily*, one of the most out of the way places in the county. The old chapel, half-timbered but restored in brick, is decorated with 17th century paintings showing the coats-of-arms of Charles II and the Mainwaring family (whose old hall was close by). The Lord's Prayer, the Creed and the Ten Commandments are also painted in this odd little church in the pastures of South Cheshire. This area has the unusual canal drawbridges based on the Dutch ones that we find in Van Gogh's paintings.

At *Wrenbury*, a charming spot with the old church by the village green, is a place where bears used to be baited. One vicar was delivering his sermon when a visiting bear arrived and both priest and congregation left the church to see the animal being paraded around the green. The old church has a quaint corner tower to carry the stairs to the top of the tower which is capped with a weather vane. It has charming box pews with painted coats-of-arms and a brass chandelier of the 18th century. There are early 19th century monuments to the Cotton and Starkey families, including one to Sir Stapleton Cotton, Viscount Combermere, a friend of Wellington. Robed figures point to the battles in which 'The Lion of Gold' (as he was called by the Spanish) took part. It is this same Viscount Combermere whose equestrian statue stands outside the gates of Chester Castle *Combermere Abbey* has long vanished, but the great house built on the site remains today in its delightful park with a lake where herons nest. It is still a private home, with memories of the days when the Empress of Austria hunted here in Queen Victoria's days.

An interesting development in these parts is the wildlife park at *Bridgemere* — no savage wild beasts here but there are birds of prey, water fowl and deer, and at *Stapely* there are fish ponds and aquaria for us to visit.

One of the loveliest villages in the county is *Marbury*. It takes its name from the two meres near the ivy clad church, which has mellowed into the surroundings. Old cottages nestle close by and we travel to it along some lovely tree-lined lanes. The 15th century timber pulpit is a thing of beauty. There is a tree, planted to commemorate Waterloo, with seats around its massive trunk outside the old *Swan Inn*, a delightful spot in the undulating country which was created when the ice sheets dropped their moraine here to form the border with Shropshire.

By Lawton Gate

(the gap in the hills at Lawton took the main road to London; a girl who gave Lawton Gate a slam left the county to go to the big city, often under doubtful circumstances)

SANDBACH is a place which was important in Saxon days. Art historians and archaeologists come to look at its two crosses and to argue and debate on their origins and their meanings. The two crosses were unlikely to have stood together when first set up but have been placed in the middle of the old cobbled square for as long as anyone can tell. They were destroyed by the Puritans and were restored by the same George Ormerod who wrote the most momentous history of Cheshire. It is possible that the crosses were set up when Peada, the son of heathen Penda married the daughter of the King of Northumbria on condition that she should be the queen of a Christian country. St. Chad and others came from Northumbria to convert Mercia. It is held by some that their Minster church was at Sandbach and the various churches to St. Chad in the county are where he preached to early converts. The first Bishop of Lichfield travelled about on foot, so that when the Archbishop of Canterbury purchased a horse for him, he refused to ride, saying that his Saviour had been content to walk. The archbishop himself lifted Chad into the saddle before he consented to ride.

Saxon stones which were once built into the base of the crosses have been moved for safety to the church. Some contend that this rich array of Saxon work indicates that there must have been great activity in Saxon times and argue it to be proof of Chad's Minster, but it must not be forgotten that Ormerod searched from end to end of the county for bits of the crosses and there is no proof that all the stonework was in Sandbach in Saxon Times.

There are interesting half-timbered buildings, not least the 17th century *Black Bear* with its thatched roof. The church itself was much restored by Scott in the 19th century and has an interesting walk-way under the tower, copied from St. Michael's at Chester. The church roof is 17th century, but the rest was renewed by Scott who was at work from 1847-9 and at whose hands many churches in Cheshire suffered restoration. Scott was travelling on a train when he saw a church being restored. He asked his assistant if he knew who was restoring the building—the assistant replied, 'Yes Sir, you are'.

Sandbach has a fine hostelry in *The Old Hall*, which looks out over the churchyard. It has good Jacobean woodwork inside and a rare set of dog-gates to prevent the household pets going upstairs. Market day on Thursdays brings visitors from all over the county. It is held on Scot's Common, so called because some of Prince Charles Stuart's following were killed and buried at the spot after the battle of Worcester. While Charles was hiding in his oak tree, they came to Sandbach on market day. Too exhausted to fight, the market crowd soon took most of them prisoners and locked them in the church.

Sandbach is well known to industrialists, as the place where Edwin Foden set up his motor works. When he died in 1964 his coffin was carried to the little church at Elworth on a steam lorry called the 'The pride of Edwin' made at his factory in 1916. Close by are the salt and chemical works by the canal and at *Moston*, where tradition says the Baron of Kinderton killed a dragon, are some stretches of water created by subsidence, now the home of waterfowl and rare plants.

A fine piece of water is the mill-pond at *Winterley* with its profusion of bird life. The road from Sandbach to Crewe runs right by its side. *Haslington* is an interesting village with some old cottages, and a small church built last century. The fine old timber Hall was built by Admiral Sir Francis Vernon who helped Drake defeat the Armada. *Hassal* was once kown for its unfinished church, on which work started but was never completed. The building was demolished before a single service was held for its builder died leaving no money to complete the works.

Alsager is known for its college opened for emergency teacher training after the 2nd World War. It has the finest classical church in Cheshire, built in 1790 for the Misses Alsager at a cost of £10,000. The church was placed under the jurisdiction of the church at Barthomley and it was not until 1946 that it became totally independent of the mother church. In the meantime a new parish church had been built to serve the town that would be free of interference from outside.

Barthomley church is unique as it is the only church dedicated to St. Bertoline, an 8th century prince who became a hermit on an island in the River Sow in Staffordshire. We remember a sad event here. On Christmas Eve 1643 Lord Byron's band of Royalists came into the village. The villagers took refuge in the tower, but the Royalists made a fire at the bottom using rushmats and church pews to smoke them out. They surrendered and came out hoping for a peaceful outcome, but they were stripped and murdered.

In carved alabaster we find Sir Robert Foulshurst, one of the four Cheshire squires who distinguished themselves at Poitiers in 1356. His feet rest on a lion and his children are on the box of the tomb. His namesake was the village priest a century later and he has a fine effigy too. The loveliest thing in this splendid church, however, is the tomb of Lady Hoghton who died in 1887. Carved by Sir Joseph Edgar Boehm, she is shown in a plain dress sleeping on a richly embroidered pillow.

By the Sandbach junction with the M6 is the late medieval Brickhouse Farm, one of the finest timbered farms in the county. It looks out over a rural landscape which has the Victorian church spire of *Sandbach Heath* as its focal point.

The Hill Country

'Congleton rare, Congleton rare,
Sold the church Bible to buy a bear.'

LOCALS still talk of this old town as bear-town, situated on the banks of the River Dane with Congleton Cloud, its very own mountain, and Mow-Cop (the bald hill) looking over it. The church is a curiosity itself, of 18th century date but replacing a much older one. It is dedicated to St. Peter ad Vincula — St. Peter in chains — and shares this rare dedication with a chapel in the Tower of London. What about the bears? Well, they tell of a time when the old bear died just before the town fair. What would Congleton Fair be without a bear baiting spectacle? Hastily the townsfolk got together and decided that it was worthwhile using the money that had been collected for a new church Bible to buy a replacement bear.

There are a few relics of the old days that have survived, including St. Peter's chains—leather belts with bells that were worn by people to advertise the chimney sweeps' holiday. There are some old silk mills and a lovely park by the River Dane. Some old houses survive, and the *Lion and Swan* is an ancient hostelry with a half-timbered upper storey but 'WOM' on one of the 17th century cottages is more likely to be the initials of the builder than the Cheshire dialect word for home.

Congleton still produces textiles and clothing, even though most of her menfolk find employment outside the town, but we come to the old town as a starting point to visit other places nearby or the part of the Peak District National Park that is in Cheshire.

At *Astbury* we find one of the finest churches in the county. It is of late 15th or early 16th century date, with a porch of three storeys where the tower should be and a tower and spire added as if they were afterthoughts. The porch roof was never given the vault it deserved, but an odd group of musicians were carved to hold it. We find a lovely group of medieval saints in stained glass, which survived because they were set too high when the Puritans broke most of the glass and destroyed the organ (in a field known to this day as organ field). Now they are set in a window close to the font, an unusual construction in itself with a cover that is counterbalanced by a device on the wall. Above it is a ceiling richly carved with angels—if we look at it from the nave we see the angels hang between the arches. The ancient craftsmen designed the roof to fit a required space and made it elsewhere taking no account of the layout of the building it was to cover.

There are ancient ceilings on the nave and the south aisle too and beautiful carvings in the screens. The church possesses a 15th century lectern carved like an eagle, the emblem of St. John the Evangelist. It grasps a globe in its claws and can be turned to face any member of the congregation that the reader feels might benefit from the text. There are old monuments, one to Lady Egerton of Elizabeth's reign and another to a knight of the Black Prince's day. On a panel high above the nave is a painting of Our Lady knighting St. George.

Outside there are gargoyles heavy and wide-mouthed, carved from the gritty stone of this part of the county. There is a yew tree which must be one of the oldest in the land; propped up in old age with a gap in the trunk wide enough to walk through, it still manages to produce green leaves. Close to it are a group of monuments in local stone, one to a knight and one to a clergyman. There is a knight and a lady under a canopy with an interesting inscription placed there after the old cavalier historian of Cheshire, Sir Peter Leycaster, caused a stir amongst the Cheshire gentry of the time. He dared to suggest that a lady called Amice was in fact a bastard daughter of Hugh Cevelioc, the 13th century Earl of Chester. She had been married in Over church, but the legitimacy of her birth was put in doubt in the 17th century after the Mainwarings of Peover adopted the Earl's coat-of-arms. Most of the local gentry were related to her and this inscription was placed there by one of them in an attempt to prove this couple to be Amice and her husband.

The gateway to the churchyard was built in the 16th century in memory of a former vicar. When the village May Queen is crowned, it is here that they place her throne. When the churchyard was extended they unearthed a Bronze Age burial urn, indicating that this place was held sacred long before the birth of Christ. The village green is charming surrounded by old houses with daffodils blooming in the spring time.

The glory of this part of the county is *Moreton Old Hall,* the finest moated half-timbered house in the realm. Richard Dale, the carpenter, placed his name on the windows here 'God is all in all things', he carved. Moreton Hall was built less than a century after Astbury church, but is different altogether. The church was built in the days before the Reformation, when all good men left their money to the Church — living in simple houses themselves with their cattle and other livestock often in the same room, a hole in the roof allowed the smoke to escape from a hearth in the centre of the floor. The hall of Moreton Hall was built in this fashion, with the pantry where the pans were stored and the buttery where the barrels (or butts) were kept at one end. We may trace the gentleman's growth in status as Thomas Moreton added extra rooms, including a drawing room where the ladies withdrew after meals while the gentlemen drank and joked. There was a gate-house, above were bedrooms, and a thing that no respectable Elizabethan house would have been without — the long gallery, for games in the day time and for balls in the evening.

Even though it made Little Moreton look like the creation of a fairy tale writer, it *had* to have its long gallery. Chimneys were added to the old hall — they were the height of fashion and were constructed in 'new fangled' brick. A window existed before they were built and a hole was left to allow light to enter.

No great house of that time would have been complete without its solar windows and, not to be outdone, William Moreton built two into a corner of the courtyard. They are so close together that the upper storeys form a bridge from one room to the next. There are old fireplaces and a room which is entered by a sliding panel in the wainscot work: not because it was a hideaway, but merely because it was fashionable to have a secret place.

The oak wainscot panels at Little Moreton are very fine and practical. They could be taken down and installed elsewhere if the family moved, and in one of the rooms at Moreton we find a partition wall made from panels taken from some other part of the house. The long gallery must have been splendid when it was lit by candles for a great ball. Seen over the dark Cheshire plain, the long wall of glass must have looked like a great lantern and been reflected in sparkling ripples on the moat. Visitors today get little idea of the original layout of the house, for it is unfurnished for the most part. It retains, however, a fascination largely by virtue of its quaint twisted walls, its many gables and its long gallery perched above the moat.

Moreton Hall is a monument to the newly rich of Tudor England. Moreton spent his time wisely collecting wealth, purchasing land and avoiding political troubles. The only time he is recorded in the official records was when he took his neighbours from Rode Hall to court, to settle a dispute about who should sit nearer to the front and go first in processions at Astbury church. This was no petty matter. It established for everyone to see who should take precedence. The nearer to the front a person sat, the more important he was; by establishing this and by creating the great house, he told the whole world in no uncertain terms what his status was. Religion still played an important part in his life and there is a delightful private chapel rich with Renaissance paintings, restored early this century. Services are still held from time to time. A charming detail of the courtyard is a kennel built into the walls with a stone dog bowl.

In the distance we see *Mow Cop*, its sham ruin built as a summer-house for Randle Wilbraham, the owner of Rode Hall, now in the care of the National Trust. The hill stands on the border with Staffordshire and on May 31st, 1807, it was the site of the first camp meeting of what was to become the Primitive Methodist Church. Called by Hugh Bourne of Longton, the meeting created a revivalist image inspired by the American movements of the time. They were expelled by the Methodist Conference and set up their own movement. Many years went by before the various branches reunited to form the church that we know today. The Methodists still climb this wild hillside to hold services from time to time.

When they built the 'castle' on the hill, someone made a mistake in the position and it was found to be partly on the Rode Hall estate and partly on a neighbour's land. They of course objected, and the matter was taken to court. The judge ruled that the castle could stay as long as both parties had a key and both could make use of it.

On another high-land spot in this part of the world we find the *Bridestones*. They are the remains of a prehistoric tomb, perhaps 4,000 years old. They stand on a hilltop with their entrance facing away from the Cheshire plain, indicating that those who built it preferred the highlands and lived further up the hills. Visitors are usually loathe to leave for there is a strange peace about the spot where our early ancestors cremated their dead. The tomb has been proved to be linked with the Irish burial mounds and it is probable that some wandering band of tribesmen crossed the Irish Sea, travelled this way via the Mersey, Weaver and Dane to set up camp on this grand hillside looking out over the Cheshire Plain. The Romans left little evidence of their presence. Recently, however, a fortress large enough for a legion to camp has been found at Bent Farm, Astbury, indicating a brief visit in those far off times.

The roads in the area wind through pleasant countryside, with the hills of England's backbone looking down. One of the most attractive spots is at *Gawsworth,* where the main road carries traffic away from the village, allowing it to remain largely unspoiled. The charm of Gawsworth will remain with all who have called in here. The church is reflected in a pool, with ducks and other waterfowl peacefully swimming. The church of St. James is 15th century, and has retained its sanctus bellcote at the east end where a bell was rung when mass was celebrated. The tower has a crown of pinnacles and in the churchyard is an old cross base with a new timber shaft.

The glory of Gawsworth church is in the monuments to the Fitton family, restored to their original rich colours. Gawsworth and the Fittons are synonymous and we find monuments of the first half of the 17th century to the Fittons who lived in Shakespeare's day. Dame Alice Fitton dressed in widow's weeds, rests her arm on the tomb of her husband with her hand supporting her head; her other hand rests on a closed book. She looks a sad lady who has taken all that the world could do in her stride. Her two sons·are in front and behind her daughters kneel in prayer. One of them was Mary, who was a lady in the court of Elizabeth I until she disgraced herself by bearing a child, rumoured to be that of Elizabeth's own favourite the Earl of Pembroke and was forced to return home in disgrace. Mary has greater claim to fame, as the possible mysterious 'dark lady' for whom Shakespeare penned his sonnets is believed to be no less than the wayward maid of Gawsworth. Beatrice Tunstall wrote her novel *The Dark Lady* about a 19th century Mary Fitton of Gawsworth. The old home is now open to all, carefully and lovingly looked after by Mr. and Mrs. Raymond Richards, historians themselves. Gawsworth is still a home in atmosphere. It is warm and welcoming — we feel like invited guests, not curious tourists when we walk round the rooms. The library is filled with old books, many of them about Cheshire. The bed chambers are still used, and the Richards' grand-children have been christened in the family chapel. The gardens are carefully maintained and we may also see the remains of one of the very few mediaeval tilting grounds to survive. Perhaps not surprisingly they were always known as the 'Fighting Fittons'. Even before the Fittons, people lived in this delightful spot and a stone axe of the Neolithic period has been found. Gawsworth has a collection of old coaches that are still used on its roads and the village pub is little changed since coaching days.

The old rectory of Gawsworth is one of the few houses of the period to remain as a private residence and keep its 15th century great hall much as it was in the Middle Ages. A strange possession of the National Trust near Gawsworth is a small wood, containing the grave of Maggotty Johnson — sometimes known as Lord Flame, an eccentric character claimed to be the last jester in England. He died in 1773 and was buried in the wood at his own request; his epitaph describes him:

> *Here undisturbed and hid from vulgar eyes,*
> *A wit, musician, poet, player lies.*

Lord Mohun built the new hall at Gawsworth before his famous duel with the Duke of Hamilton. Intended to decide the ownership of Gawsworth, it ended with both parties dead. One of the most famous duels in English history, it gave Thackeray the theme for part of his novel *Henry Edmond.*

From Gawsworth we travel to *Macclesfield*—the name of this town is linked always with silk and they still elect a Silk Queen. St. Michael's church stands on a hill with wide views, we come to it up 108 steps that wind their way through the old houses. Many of the streets in this old town lead uphill to the church which is situated like a castle on the hilltop. There was a castle here, but that vanished years ago. Churches dedicated to St. Michael are usually sited on hills, and this Cheshire mount of St. Michael is well worth a visit. The stalls of the market make a colourful scene by the gates, some shelter under a modern roof near the stately Town Hall with portico and columns. Much of the church was renewed last century but there are old objects inside. The chapel of the Savage family has as fine a set of monuments as any church in the North West. For those who love to study arms and armour, it is a happy hunting ground. Two Sir Johns lie under arches, one died the year that America was discovered (1492) the other in 1527. Their tombs are decorated with their shields and the crest of the family, a unicorn's head. A Sir John Savage who died in 1528 is shown with his wife, her head supported by angels and lap-dogs are playing in the folds of her dress. The monument to another John was erected in 1639, by his grandson, though he died in 1597. The builder of Rock Savage, he has a canopy with classical ladies reclining above it. His wife was of higher status and is shown a step above her husband on the tomb. The priest's quarters are like a miniature tower attached to the chapel. The original stone altar has survived with consecration crosses where it was blessed by the bishop. A strange figure has been made in two parts. The feet and head are enclosed in box-like slabs of alabaster while the pelvic region is not represented at all, a mass of cement was simply added and trowelled square.

A brass to Roger Legh of Ridge was probably moved here at some time from the Legh chapel and remounted, for the wood on which it hangs shows no sign of his wife and daughters who were once depicted in prayer with him, while his sons kneel behind him in prayer. In the centre is an illustration of a miracle of St. Gregory. An old lady challenged him for proof that the sacramental bread — which she had herself baked — was in fact the body of Christ. Gregory is shown kneeling before the altar while Christ appears to him. An inscription records that Roger Legh was pardoned for 26,000 years and 26 days for saying five Paternosters (the Lord's Prayer) and five Aves (Ave Maria)—a reference to the mediaeval practice of selling forgiveness for sins.

In a glass case are some fragments of armour from Cromwell's day found here many years ago. There is a fine monument to Earl Rivers of 1696, a descendant of the Savages who lie in the Savage chapel, he saw their fine home of Rock Savage at Runcorn destroyed in the Civil

War. A massive marble canopy with stone curtains hangs above his bewigged effigy. There are more effigies on either side of the altar, and more inscriptions in the Legh chapel, now used as a baptistry. They include one in memory of John Brownsword, who may have been Shakespeare's schoolmaster, and one to Sir Piers Legh of Lyme who was a follower of Richard II and was executed by Henry Bolingbroke at Chester. His son is recorded on the same inscription; he was at Agincourt and died at Paris before being carried back to this Cheshire hilltop. There is a grave slab of 1788 in the churchyard, which has sadly been damaged when a drain was put through a corner of it. It records Mary Broomfield who saved £5 out of her pension of ninepence a week to pay for her grand funeral in the old churchyard and thus earned herself a place amongst the worthies of Macclesfield.

The Georgian church of Macclesfield is Christ Church, founded by Charles Roe, one of the first silk mill owners, determined to have a tower on his church that would be higher than that of St. Michael's. As his church stood on lower ground, his architect was forced to create a disproportionately high tower and even prophesied that it would fall down as soon as the bells were rung. It survived however and remains today an interesting monument of the days of self-made men in our industrial history.

It was silk that created the Macclesfield that we know and some of the fine old mills with their rows of large windows still survive, though they are now used for other purposes as little silk is made today since it has been replaced by man made fibres. The mills are not the only architectural remains of Macclesfield silk. Many of the houses have a long window let into the roof, they were the weaver's windows. They provided light to a loft where the loom worked when Macclesfield silk was a cottage industry. It was the moist atmosphere of the hills that was conducive to silk manufacture and made Macclesfield and Congleton silk towns. Reminders of the silk industry may be found in the museum in West Park where exhibits of the old trade are shown. There are also treasures from Egypt and the East and a brank — an iron object used to punish scolding or gossiping women. A sedan chair moved from St. Michael's was given by Catherine Roe (the daughter of Charles who built Christ Church) for the use of aged or infirm parishioners. The museum was given in Victoria's Diamond Jubilee year, 1897 (an account published at the time could be used as a guide today) by the Brocklehurst family, whose home, Swythamley Hall, is today a centre for transcendental meditation.

In the park we find three cross shafts from Saxon times, they are round and show the influence of the Danes who settled hereabouts. Two had been used as gateposts before being carried here for safety. A great boulder said to weigh 30 tons was carried here by the flowing ice of the Ice Age. Macclesfield is a typical Northern mill town. In the good beer guide we read that it has more than 60 'real ale' pubs, many in back streets. It has also a large Sunday School of 1813 built to provide elementary education for the workers.

Macclesfield Forest was a forest largely without trees for in the past 'Forest' was a legal term indicating a Royal hunting area. They say that the last wolf in England was killed here and there is the quaintly named *Wildboarclough,* reminding us of the hunting which once took place. The village pub is called the *Wild Boar.* In the little village of Macclesfield Forest is a simple stone chapel built in the 17th century and renewed in the 19th, where they still perform rush-bearing services when gaily decorated carts bring rushes to scatter on the floor.

Few people who visit these wild hillsides will want to miss the famous *Cat and Fiddle,* 1,600 ft. above sea level. It is the second highest inn in the land and is said to keep alive the name of a loyal forester of these parts called Catton Fidelis (the faithful). It was claimed that when poachers from Derbyshire came this way, they were captured by Catton who smiled with such satisfaction that it gave rise to the saying to 'grin like a Cheshire cat'.

Whalley Bridge is on the road from Macclesfield to the pretty village of Rainow. It has a three century old pub *The Highwayman* in a superb setting. In the winter we half expect to meet the highwayman when we come this way by night. *Wincle* is an out of the way place with old houses of stone in the Pennine tradition where a hoard of Roman gold jewellery was found last century. It is now a treasured possession of the British Museum. The wild Derbyshire border is an interesting place to explore, the wild moorlands having a character unlike the Cheshire Plain with old gritstone cottages and drystone walls. The National Trust maintains the oddly named Tegg's Nose and Eddisbury Park Field for the public, but there is splendid moorland with lovely cloughs and wide views to explore in all parts of the border.

On Manchester's Doorstep

THE new county of Greater Manchester took over much that had formerly been part of Cheshire, but the area on the boundaries, still in Cheshire, is of considerable interest. Not inappropriately we start at *Lyme.* The very name may be derived from Limes — the boundary in Latin and it was Lyme that was the borderland between Cheshire and Derbyshire. They say that it was the Derbyshire men who came down to raid the rich lands of Cheshire who coined the saying:

> *Cheshire born Cheshire bred,*
> *Strong in th'arm — weak in th'yed.*

Cheshire men changed this to 'Quick in th'yed' (quick-witted). No doubt the Derby men had felt the strong arm. The old hall at Lyme stands at a higher altitude than any other great house in the country. The facade is Georgian with Palladian columns and is capped by statues of classical gods overlooking a lake. There are some exquisite carvings by the greatest English woodcarver, Grinling Gibbons, but the majority of the house is Elizabethan, particularly the Stag-Parlour with scenes of the Lyme tradition of driving deer over the water in plaster work as a frieze above the wainscot panels. There is a painting of 'The Black Prince' hinged so that observers could look down on visitors in the hall below. Above the stairs is a plaster ceiling showing an arm with a banner recalling that an ancestor saved the Black Prince's banner from falling into the hands of the French. We remember two sad figures from England's history; Mary Queen of Scots spent some of her captivity here and Charles I is shown in a portrait with his death warrant in his hand. Such portraits of the end of the Martyr King were popular. Vale Royal once boasted a portrait of him putting on his execution cap. There are chairs at Lyme covered with fabric from a cloak he once wore. A portrait of the little princes and princesses of Spain by Velazquez is exhibited in print form here; their pet, one of the famous Lyme mastiffs, is shown with them. The park still has its herd of deer, although the famous Lyme white cattle are now extinct — a sad loss as they are believed to have been similar to those kept by prehistoric man.

A visit to Lyme starts with the fun of riding from the gates in a small 'train' pulled by a tractor. In the park is the grim 'cage' said to be where poachers were locked up; it no doubt acted as a watch — or pele — tower in times of border trouble. At *Lyme Handley* are the Bowstones, Anglo-Nordic cross shafts whose heads are in the hall at Lyme.

Disley is close by, a lovely area with cloughs and small streams tumbling from the highlands. The attraction of Disley lies in its setting in the hills. Its old church rich with old glass imported from the continent, has a lovely roof with a host of angels carved in wood.

Adlington Hall has a fine Palladian facade with tall columns and a portico, but it also has a black and white courtyard of Elizabethan days. At Utkinton Hall a single tree stands as a column with its roots in the ground. At Adlington two trees have been left to form the main supports of the Great Hall. Its canopy, where the lord of the manor's table would have been, is rich with coats-of-arms of the various families who had intermarried with this branch of the Leghs. There are paintings of the Restoration years on the walls and a charming view of the hall is gained from the minstrels gallery. The old organ is the only one in the country on which 18th century music may be played and sound as it did when Handel came here and composed 'The Harmonious Blacksmith' on this same keyboard after a visit to the local smithy. A copy of his manuscripts is still exhibited. The organ stands in a gallery between the two old trees. The trunks have been hewn with an adze to form columns with Gothic panels while the roof is a fine hammer-beam with carved angels looking down.

One of the most notable of the Leghs was Sir Uryan, one of the Englishmen who 'singed the King of Spain's beard' and was knighted by Elizabeth for his services at Cadiz. He captured a Spanish lady whom he treated with such courtesy that she gave him a gold chain. His portrait hangs in the hall with the chain clearly shown. Adlington village is charming and noted today for its folk dancers who tour the county giving demonstrations.

Prestbury is one of Cheshire's best known villages, an attractive place where the wealthy choose to live. Its name is interpreted as 'Priests. Town' and one of its most charming buildings is the old Priest's House. There is a balcony over the door from which the Puritan incumbent preached when he was banished from the church.

In the churchyard is a Saxon cross in a glass case. There is also one of the most perfect Norman chapels in the North West. Much of it was rebuilt in the 18th century but the facade is original, with a door under a Norman rounded arch with rich mouldings. A carving in the half-moon shaped tympanum above once showed Christ in Glory with the symbols of the Apostles around him. Above are figures which would have been saints when the chapel was new, but which have weathered into almost meaningless lumps of stone.

The church of Prestbury is rich in flat Tudor alabaster slabs with inscribed pictures of the Downs, Worth and Warren families. 18th century paintings of the Apostles look down on the worshippers from above the arches, while there is 17th century work in the pulpit. Much of the church is 13th century in date, but the font with its odd faces may well be Norman. There are some interesting epitaphs in the churchyard, including one to Maria Rathbone:-

> *Thrice helpless child, thus doomed to roam,*
> *And leave thy every friend at home.*

The story of Maria caused as much of a stir in these parts as the murder of Maria Marten in the Red Barn. She was aged eight years when she lost her way and wandered away from the village. She was found in a field near the *Crown Inn* at Peover after a search lasting 25 days. She was lost in December and a violent storm with thunder and snow put an end to her wanderings and her life.

A stone of 1750 tells its own story:-

> *Beneath this stone lies Edward Green*
> *Who for cutting stone famous was seen,*
> *But he was sent to aprehend*
> *One Joseph Clarke of Kerridge End*
> *For stealing deer of Esquire Downes,*
> *When he was shot and died O'the wounds.*

The river Bollin sparkles by the side of the *Admiral Rodney Inn* while *The Legh Arms*, formerly known as the *Black Boy*, is 17th century and tradition has it that Bonnie Prince Charlie was a guest.

Pot Shringley is a lovely mountain village. The ancient church has interesting glass, fine woodwork and old pews which were made for Gawsworth and came here 'second hand'. In his will dated June 7th, 1492 — the year that Columbus sailed to America — Geoffrey Downes left money to found the church, stipulating that the priest should keep 'Noe horse, Ne hawke, ne hounde' as these might divert him from service to God. He also stipulated that if the priest told tales about his neighbours he would lose the living, he 'would rather have no priest than one that was an enemy of God'. We feel little has changed since the days when Geoffrey founded his chapel here. The valley where several glens meet is well wooded and it is an attractive drive through winding highland lanes to find it. A college in this remote place trains priests of the Catholic church, who might be reminded of Geoffrey Downes' stipulations on what made a good priest almost 500 years ago.

A fine vantage-point here is *Kerridge End* with the tower of White Nancy, erected to mark the victory of Waterloo, overlooking the valley of the river Dean. Below is *Bollington,* an old cotton town with a few mills still in existence. A viaduct of twenty arches carries the railway over the valley and there are wide views into Derbyshire. It is a pleasant little town with many of its houses built of local grey gritstone and roofed with the famous Kerridge flagstones.

Just off the main Manchester/Chester road, not far from where it joins the busy M56, is the delightful village of *Rostherne.* We turn off down a side lane and travel into another world. I have been here on an autumn or winter evening when the leaves are golden or the trees are black and leafless and on spring evenings when all is bright and new. To come to this churchyard is a never-ending delight, for it looks over Rostherne Mere. We are not allowed to go too close as it is a nature reserve, but the spectacle from the churchyard is one of ever-changing loveliness. The mere is a rest point for flocks of migrating birds; it attracts gulls by the thousand who fly in from all parts at evening so that the sky is sometimes a veritable snow storm. Geese swim on the water and those with field glasses can pick out most unusual species, and you may even spot a mermaid.

The story tells that when they were hanging bells in the church, one of them fell causing the workmen to swear. Thus defiled the bell was no longer fit for the house of God and rolled down into the mere. They tried in vain to retrieve it. They say that a mermaid keeps the bell as a plaything and from time to time she can be heard ringing it under the water. Certainly the mere has many secrets. It was formed by natural subsidence into an underground brine spring thousands of years ago and from its depths a kind of fish only found in sea water (apart from here) used to be caught before a protection order for all wildlife was made. There are tales of an underwater passage linking Rostherne to the sea. It is a romantic place and it is refreshing in these busy days to find this little haven of peace and tranquillity, where we remember the activities of the Cheshire naturalists Major Boyd and T. A. Coward.

Rostherne's most splendid treasure is a tomb to Charlotte Lucy Beatrix Egerton. According to the historians she died of a 'broncial affliction in 1845 aged 21', but a local tradition says she drowned in the mere on the eve of her wedding. Charlotte lies on her side in a thin dress — said to be her wedding gown — while a white marble angel leans over her with wings outstretched.

An interesting effigy is believed to be a Venables crusader of the time of Henry III. His stone coffin is now placed outside the church — what happened to his body is not recorded. The monument was found when the church tower fell down in 1741. There is a helmet and gauntlets on the chancel wall belonging to some long-departed knight and in the churchyard a massive monument in the style of the Albert Memorial. The churchyard gate has a wooden ball which acts as a counter weight to close it after us, a job it has been performing since 1640. We also remember Adam Martindale — a fiery Puritan who was sent away from here after he cut down the village maypole because the villagers 'had profaned the Sabbath with musick and dancing' in honour of 'the strumpet Flora in Rome'.

By leafy lanes we come to *Mobberley*, a wide spread village with the quaint pub-name *The Frozen Mop* to remind those who come in summer that the climate can turn cool. *The Roebuck Inn* reminds us that 'you can tell a Mobberley man by his breeches' because they would be made of buckskin from a night's poaching in Tatton Park. When it rains they say:

It rains it pains, it patters i'th docks,
'cos Mobberley wenches is washin' their socks.

The old rectory was the home of the Mallory family from 1795 to 1885. The east window was set up in memory of one of them who was rector for over half a century. There is, however, a more striking window set up in memory of the most famous of them. George Mallory is remembered by the inscription,

All his life he sought after whatsoever things
are pure and high and eternal. At last in the flower
of his perfect manhood, he was lost to human sight
between earth and heaven on the topmost peak of Everest.

The hero of all school-boys a generation or two ago, when asked why he wanted to climb Everest, he replied 'because it is there'. In the window we see Everest with two figures looking up to the peak. Mallory was lost to sight in 1924 with his younger companion, Andrew Irvine, son of the Cheshire Antiquarian W.R. Irvine. Irvine the athlete is remembered in Northwich, where an oar is a prize at the regatta each year. The window has St. George, Arthur and Galahad, a portrait of Mallory dressed as a knight kneeling at an altar, and we see the passing of Arthur, St. George and the dragon too. Sadly, Asia also claimed the Mallory's other son; Sir Trafford Leigh-Mallory was a soldier airman, killed when his plane crashed into a mountain in 1944.

The church is dedicated to St. Wilfred and a lovely window in memory of the Galloway family shows Eddi, priest of St. Wilfred, the subject of a poem by Rudyard Kipling. He held a midnight service but no-one attended, only an ox and an ass appeared and Eddi conducted his service for them,

> *How shall I tell which is greatest,*
> *How shall I tell which is least,*
> *That is my father's business,*
> *Said Eddi, St. Wilfred's priest.*

The church has retained many of its old fittings, including a splendid old screen with a loft above, installed in 1500 and richly carved. There are some old stained glass shields of local families and a gruesome 16th century painted memorial to remind us that death will come to all. An angel choir with instruments looks down on us, their wings outspread as they hold the roof in place. The bell-ringers have a gallery under the tower with an ornate screen of 1683, with Stuart period decoration. The church retains its mediaeval wall-paintings and has oil lamps on the walls.

There is an ancient yew tree in the churchyard reminiscent of Mobberley's old hall with its famous yew hedge, and there is a set of stocks hidden away in the shadow of the yew trees overlooking an inn which may have provided a few occupants in the days when too much drink could result in 'cooling one's heels' in the stocks. A peaceful spot is the old Quaker graveyard where those who rejected the order of the Church of England were buried. A tale told here is of ghosts seen in the graveyard late at night which turned out to be the slime trails left by snails on the grave stones, sparkling in car headlights. Mobberley is one of the largest parishes in England. Undulating lanes and pretty old houses make it one of the most pleasing spots on Manchester's doorstep.

There are charming lanes to explore and fine old inns hereabouts, for the pub-lunch has now-a-days replaced the 'farmhouse tea and scones' trade of the pre-war days. It is in the old ale-houses that one will sometimes meet real characters who know their village well; taken with a pinch of salt their memories will serve better than a village guide book. The old hostelries are places of historic and architectural interest themselves, and an enjoyable drive to an old village with its pub is an interesting way to spend a bright summer evening. A drive in these parts is worthwhile in these days of pre-packed food for the number of farms which sell their own produce to motorists; fresh eggs and farm potatoes—everyone knows that 'new Cheshires' are the best money can buy around here. In recent years there has been a development in self picking strawberry sales too.

The area is also one which has been settled by Manchester's commuters. Victorian merchants' houses at Alderley and Bowdon have their social and architectural interest today and I wonder if the 'ideal homes' of the mid-20th century at *Mere*, close to the golf course, will deserve preservation orders in a century's time!

Along the Bollin

THE valley of the Bollin now forms much of the north-west boundary of Cheshire. *Styal* near Wilmslow was left to the National Trust when the old mill closed down. It was felt that the wooded valley, close to Manchester, would be a pleasant place for days out in the country. Today our interest is in the social history for in the valley we find the Quarry Bank Mill. Built in 1784 by the Gregg family for the spinning of cotton it was extended in the early 19th century. Neither dark nor satanic today, having rows of large windows for the workers, the old part has three brass fire insurance plaques, since no one firm would take responsibility for it. The mill stands above a long tunnel to carry water away from the great water wheel. The manager's house is by the mill and it is possible to trace remains of a device of floats that rang a bell so that, if the water level rose too high in the night, it would wake him and remind him to open the sluice gates. A trust has been set up to develop a textile museum in the old mill.

The village of Styal is like a set for a film about Victorian England. There are rows of old cottages built for the workers and here and there are cruck cottages that were here before the Greggs came; even the village shop is the one that they built for the workers. One row of cottages was converted from an old Dutch barn, the stanchions can still be made out. Styal has memories of days before laws were passed to control the employment of children. The Apprentice House, which housed around 100 young boys and girls, is still standing. It has bars at the windows, partly to stop the apprentices from running away and partly to stop rival industrialists taking the nearly trained apprentices away. The Greggs were not unreasonable employers by the standards of the day, they were amongst the first to introduce medical help for their employees. Two young apprentices of 1806 ran away and walked to London. They were apprehended and taken before the magistrates. The boys admitted they had not been too dissatisfied with their treatment and described the way in which they were given new clothes from time to time when the old ones wore out and a Sunday suit every two years. Sunday was their day off and they spent the morning in church and the afternoon at school. Sunday schools in those days gave elementary education to working children on their free day.

An old mill worker described how he started work as a child in Styal, when the working day began at six. Each child had a piece of home-made bread at 5.30, oatmeal porridge was served at 8.30 and at 1.0 they had a half hour break for a lunch of potatoes and bacon

The Rows, one of the best-known features of Chester.

A dramatic subsidence at Northwich as a result of salt workings
[Author's collection].

The 17th century 'Black Bear' at Sandbach is notable for its half-timbering and thatched roof.

The immense sweep of the Cheshire Plain as viewed from near Beeston Castle.

A characteristic wooded glade in Delamere Forest.

Mostyn House School and the promenade at Parkgate, Wirral.

Opening the lock gates at Tilstone Lock, Shropshire Union Canal.

The magnificent Norman chapel at Prestbury which boasts a richly carved facade.

The obelisk at Farndon recalls Roger Barnston, who during the Crimean War led the campaign to relieve Lucknow.

The "Alice window" at Daresbury church, a memorial to Charles Lutwidge Dodgeson—better known by his pen name, Lewis Carroll.

Gawsworth old rectory, a private residence which retains its 15th century great hall.

The Cat & Fiddle Inn, 1,600 feet above sea level on the borders of Cheshire and Derbyshire.

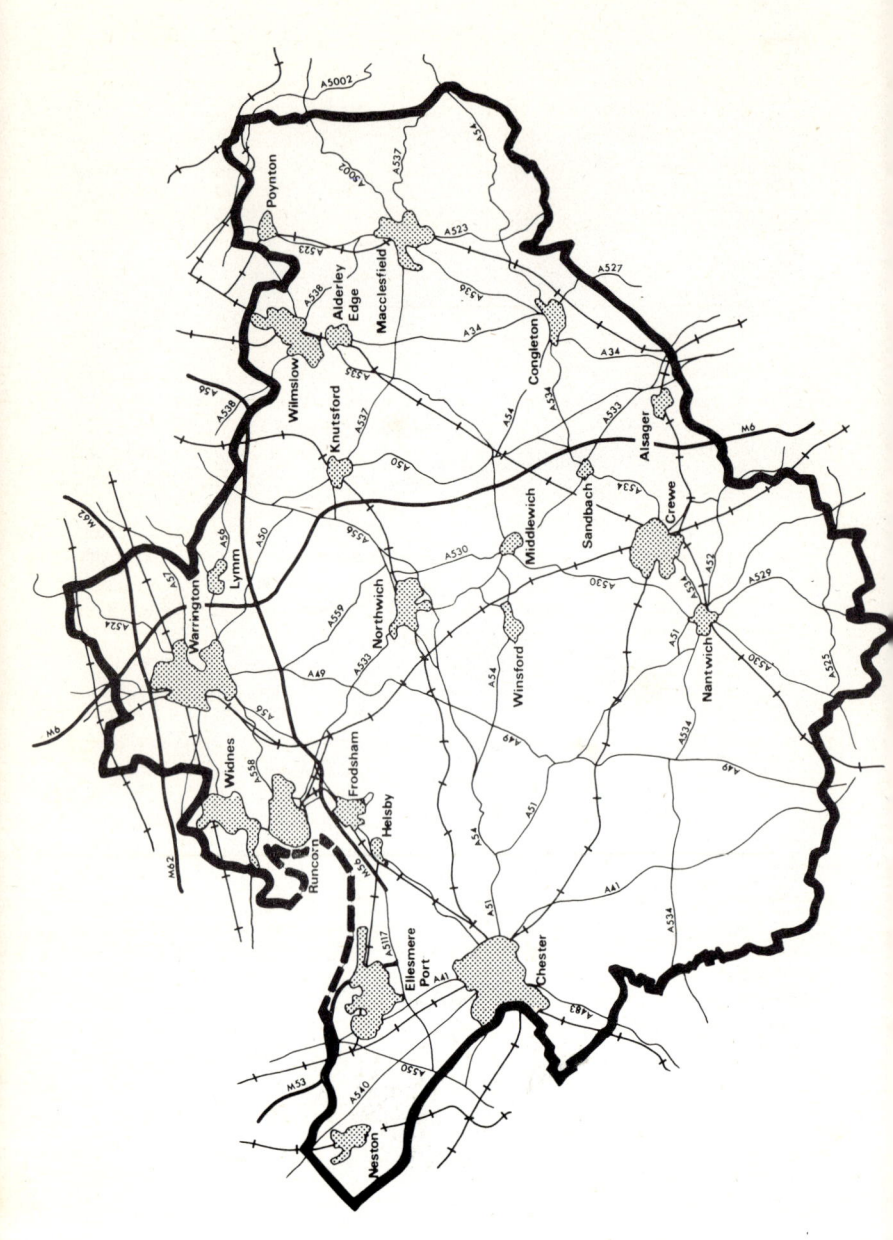

from the farms on the estate. A snack at half past five broke the afternoon and work continued until 8.30 pm.

At *Nether Alderley* is the old corn mill looking as if it has grown out of the hillside; it has a long low roof with Kerridge slabs covered in mosses. The mill has great wheels that drive the old timber machinery. There is a lovely feel about the place enhanced by the sound of bumping machines. Corn is still ground here on the days that the mill is open. A splendid example of mediaeval economics, the mill pond is also the moat of the old manor house while the long slope of the roof was ideal to collect rain water via a tub at the corner.

Alderley is the village of the Stanley family and their crest was an eagle and child. A lovely old cottage was formerly an inn of that name. Sir Thomas Lathom, in the time of King Edward III, had no heir to continue the line. He was, however, the father of an illegitimate son and legitimate daughter. He told his wife about a dream in which he found a child stolen by an eagle. Afterwards he arranged for his son to be placed at the foot of a tree in which there was an eagle's nest; walking that way with his wife, he pretended to find the child, deceiving his wife who adopted the boy. He was given the name of the mother, Sir Oscatel Lathom. Shortly before his death, however, Sir Thomas decided to make a full confession, so Oscatel did not inherit. In the meantime the daughter had married one of the Stanleys who adapted Thomas' crest, which showed an eagle with a child. The Stanley arms, from ill-feeling towards Oscatel, became an eagle preying on a child.

Cheshire is linked with many Arthurian legends. The tale of *Sir Gawain and the Green Knight* was written for the Mascies of Dunham (a former part of Cheshire) and the Green Knight is finally found by Gawain in the Wirral. The theme of the Green Knight belongs to a Celtic fertility cult — we find him in many a Cheshire church as a carved head with vegetation growing from him. He is the old pre-Christian sacrifice, killed and buried in the spring to ensure the growth of crops. It is said that Chester was Caerleon — the 'Castle of Legions' that was to become King Arthur's Camelot when the Romans departed.

There are more ancient stories around Alderley. Legend tells of the farmer from Mobberley taking a fine white horse to sell at Macclesfield market. An old man stopped him, said the horse would not be sold, and offered him coins he did not recognise in exchange for the animal. The farmer refused and proceeded to market, but though many came to admire, none would buy. Sad and confused the farmer was returning home when he saw the old man again. This time the farmer agreed to sell and was taken to a part of Alderley Edge where the stone opened and the old man led the farmer through stone gates to a great cavern. A round table was in the midst, and around it were seats, each occupied by a knight apart from one where a king sat. All were fast asleep. Also fast asleep were horses, one to each seat except for one, and it was here that the horse was placed. The old man explained that the knights were to sleep here until the time that England needed them most. The Edge is full of underground passages, which no doubt gave rise to the stories of secret caverns. Copper has been mined here from the Bronze Age; both Manchester and Warrington Museums exhibit stone hammers used for crushing the ore in those far off days. The mines have been used intermittently since, the last time during a copper shortage in the First World War. The Wood Mine is used by caving clubs as a training ground, around which parties may be guided to see the underground marvels. The Engine vein is reputed to be the oldest mine on the Edge. An inn called the *Wizard of the Edge* recalls the legend and is on the spot where tradition says the wizard met the farmer. An interesting place to drink is the Queensgate, where old shopfronts from the district have been built into the walls to form an alleyway of the gaslight era.

The Edge has become a centre for witchcraft. Unfortunately the witches attract others who come out of curiosity and today ambulances stand by at Hallowe'en to cope with those who lose their way and meet with accidents in the dark. The Edge is of interest to the social historian too, for in the late 19th and early 20th centuries it became a commuter settlement for Manchester businessmen who travelled daily by train. The Gothic villas that they built in splendid grounds are a feature of the district.

Nether Alderley has much of interest for those who can draw themselves away from the Edge with its wide views, its monument where the beacon told people hereabouts of the defeat of the Spanish Armada and its splendid woodlands. In the old church is the pew of the Stanleys — looking like an opera box — complete with the eagle and child crest (known in Cheshire as the 'brid and babby'). The Stanleys stood on the side at the battle of Bosworth as onlookers, and joined Henry when it was clear that Richard III had been defeated. They gained preference under the Tudors and the family is now that of Lord Derby. The letters of Lady Stanley in the 18th century have been published and form an interesting insight into the social life of the time (*The Ladies of Alderley*). Dean Stanley of Westminster restored the old abbey, finding the bones of dishonoured monarchs and acted as a guide to all. He doubtless knew all the interesting corners of the village, including the old church and school. In the churchyard is the impressive mausoleum of the family; their old home, though, has passed to the hands of I.C.I. Ltd., who use it as an experimental laboratory. The churchyard has an ancient yew tree reputed to be more than a thousand years old and the steps of an old cross are on one of the roadsides. A story of body-snatching is told here; the date was 1830 and when the two men responsible were brought before the local justices of the peace it was found that the statute books had no law against the practice. The best that could be done was a charge of trespass and of theft — one of the bodies was wearing a wedding ring and therefore it could be claimed they had stolen that.

One of the most interesting buildings to see is at *Birtles* where there is an ivy covered church with an unusual octagonal tower. Built as a chapel by the Hibberts of Birtles Hall in 1840, it was given by them in 1890 to be a parish church. The church is rich in Hibbert gifts. They were travellers who brought back interesting continental work to enrich the little church so that it has become a treasure house. There is old continental stained glass made in the Low Countries in the 17th century and there is a pulpit from the same place with the date 1655 carved on it. There are splendid old wood carvings: old chairs, an ancient eagle lectern and turned altar rails.

Wilmslow is the main town of this area having won its fight to stay in Cheshire in 1974. It has a fine selection of shops to encourage visitors; Finnegans department store moved out of Manchester to provide a specialist service in the area. Nearby is a park with the caravan home of the early broadcaster of rural matters, 'Romany'. It is open for us to view and must surely rate as the most unusual of homes open to the public. There are old houses by Lindow Common and there is one of the earliest Unitarian Chapels in the district at Dean Row. The parish church dates back to the 13th century and has a touching monumental brass. Robert Booth and his wife Dulcie lie with one hand each raised in prayer—the other hand holds the spouse's. Such a scene makes one think that this must surely have been a love match, but they were married when they were just children, she being nine and he twelve. They are shown in the dress of the 15th century. An interesting pun is found in an effigy under an arch. Humphrey Newton rests his head on three barrels, recalling that his wife was a Fitton and she is shown next to him while his mother was a Sutton. 'Tun' is an old name for barrels and the knight therefore rests on three tuns. The old badge of Congleton used the same pun, with a barrel between two conger eels. The windows of Wilmslow were once filled with old glass and some fragments still remain. There are some examples of old woodwork, including a chest carved from a solid tree trunk. An old font stands disused in the churchyard, a silent reminder of times gone by.

This is an area of contrasts, Styal is also known for its women's prison and nearby is the great complex of *Ringway*, Manchester's airport linking the North West with all parts of the world. We may visit it to see the planes come and go, or we may fly from this pleasant corner of England to every continent.

At *Great Warford* is an interesting Baptist chapel, founded in 1668 by some of Cromwell's soldiers who had settled here. In 1712 they converted a farm house into the chapel that is still used. The picturesque building still has its original Kerridge flag roof and timber frame, but the wattle and daub has been replaced with 'brick nogging'. There are old leaded windows and an inscription 'NOTHE 4 1712' probably indicating that it was number 4 chapel in the district. Baptists from the chapel at Hill Cliffe near Warrington, where Cromwell himself worshipped, came to their aid in founding the congregation. A small piece of land in Mottram St. Andrew is the chapel's burial ground.

Perhaps it is best to finish our tour of this part of the county by mentioning two fine old halls. *Chorley Hall* stands in a large moat by the roadside and it is still a home. Two houses for two branches of the family were built together to look like one large house. Here we have the 14th century hall in stone — one of the finest old halls in the land, with 17th century mullioned windows added later. A half-timbered wing of the 16th century is richly timbered with elaborate work in the gables as if it is attempting to outdo the older house in trying to gain our attention. It is open to the public. *Handforth Hall* is but a shadow of itself. Standing empty and boarded against vandals, it was once the home of the Breretons. Built by the great uncle of Sir William Brereton, it still bears his name over the door. Sir William was said to have had more to do with the downfall of Charles I than Cromwell himself. When he lived here there were more than forty rooms, not to mention outbuildings. An interesting feature of the building is a set of 'Pitt's paintings' the name given to windows painted over to look like windows but to avoid the window tax. They are on each side of two projecting bays.

By the Telescope

JODRELL BANK is known the world over, the great radio telescope is seen for miles. It tracked the first space flights and the first moon landings. There is now a selection of telescopes and other equipment on view, and the grounds are well maintained by the University of Manchester as their Botanical Gardens. There is a special attraction for visitors in the form of a planetarium where we may be instructed in star gazing. Exhibitions, cafes and other facilities help to make the visit to this modern wonder both informative and pleasurable. The name recalls an old Cheshire family who lived here long ago. Their graves are in the churchyard at the village of *Goostrey*, noted for its gooseberry shows in local pubs during the summer. The church is a good example of a Georgian brick church built in 1792 replacing an earlier half-timbered one. The village has seen much growth in recent years as its railway makes it convenient commuter country.

A charming spot to visit is *Swettenham*. Winding lanes lead to it, via a ford, which gives a thrill to the car-borne children of today. I remember coming this way on a bike and having to dismount part way through! Above the brook is the church with a fragment of Saxon carving and some vestiges of early half-timbering. It was given a new tower in the 18th century and much rebuilt a century later. Keeping it company is the *Swettenham Arms,* a country pub favoured by people from nearby towns.

Also much visited is the picturesque old water-powered saw mill in a valley, known as *Daffodil Dell.* During the spring the wooded banks of the mill pool blossom with thousands of wild daffodils. Every so often there is a display of popular feeling when proposals are renewed to flood the valley as a reservoir.

The river Dane flows peacefully along its meandering way here by *Holmes Chapel* where the church tower has marks on its base from a Civil War skirmish. The tower is mediaeval, but the body of the church is planned on Georgian lines with galleries all round. The mediaeval wooden columns and the fine 14th century roof still remain, saved for us because the Georgian builders put in plaster ceilings to hide it. An interesting feature of the church is a peg in the porch where the incumbent could hang his saddle. The busy crossroads has ceased to be the bottle-neck it was before the M6 was built when the old inns here served as welcome rest points. *The Red Lion Inn* has a window engraved by the diamond ring of a supporter of Bonny Prince Charlie who passed this way.

Cotton Hall by the road to Middlewich is a fine old timber hall, now a farm house. Railway enthusiasts will admire the railway viaduct with 23 arches each 60 ft wide and up to 105 ft high. The old village has much modern housing development, but there are still some old cottages here and there.

A well known hostelry is the *Bears Head* at *Brereton,* built in the 16th century it has a stuffed bear's head above the door. The village is known as Brereton cum Smethwick, and memorials to families of the two names are found in the church. William Smethwick and his wife, who lived just before the Civil war broke out, are shown as portrait busts. The monument was set up in William's lifetime and the date of his death was added in slightly smaller letters after the event in 1643. This fine old church also contains the memorial of William Brereton who died in 1618, his spurs, gauntlets, helmet and surcoat hang above.

The enchanting picture of Brereton is one which will long live with those who come this way. The 15th century church stands near the 16th century house, built for the heiress of the Savages of Rocksavage when she married a Brereton and is a copy of the house at Runcorn. Today it is a girls' private boarding school. *Bagmere* was famous in days gone by as the scene of the death omen. Trees floated to the surface shortly before the owner of Brereton Hall died — perhaps this was the reason why the mere was drained?

Marton church is one of Cheshire's rare treasures — it is much as it was when it was built in the 14th century. An old oak tree, said to be 1,000 years old at least, is an attraction in its own right. It saw its companions felled when Sir John de Davenport built the church and in 1370 granted 60 acres of land for the maintenance of a priest to pray for his soul. There are sandstone effigies here reputed to be Sir

John and his son Vivian. Inside, the church is a wonder of woodcraft and those who climb to the church belfry will be amazed at the intricate carpentry involved in its construction.

The Davenports were the foresters of Macclesfield forest and their gruesome crest of a felon's head with a rope around his neck is still to be seen on some of the estate houses. They, like the Dones of Utkinton, ruled the forest with a rod of iron in the Middle Ages. It is said that for each felon they executed, they received a Dee salmon from the earl. This ensured that there was no shortage of executions as the life of an innocent man was little compared with a salmon for dinner in those days! Bramall Hall, their ancient home now in Greater Manchester, is well worth a visit.

They were the ancestors of several branches of Davenports, one side of the family have opened their house to the public. *Capesthorne Hall* stands in a fine park with lakes which attract fishermen and a cumulus where some long forgotten Bronze Age chieftain lies. The house has rich collections of paintings, sculpture, and silver with a selection of Greek vases. It was built in 1722, but altered in the 19th century and almost completely rebuilt by Salvin after a disastrous fire in 1861. The house has two rooms containing early American furnishings and there is a small private theatre where the family present plays from time to time. Charlotte Davenport (1756-1859) was a proud beauty, painted by Romney and Lawrence. She banished the chaplain of Capesthorne from his pulpit after an unfortunately poor sermon the week before. She stood up as he was about to climb into the pulpit saying coolly, 'We will not trouble you for a discourse this morning'. The old chapel, a contrast to the neo-Jacobean house with its towers and turrets, was built by John Ward in 1722. His daughter Penelope married Davis Davenport, from whom the Bromley Davenports are descended. Inside the chapel is rich with plasterwork, the manorial pew is at the west end and the rest of the pews face across as was customary with a private estate chapel. There are some items on show in the house including old documents which recall the Davenports' days of power in the forest. The 'paradise bed' is hung with Elizabethan embroideries showing Adam and Eve in the Garden, their fall and expulsion. The needlework will repay examination, as the foliage is found to be alive with insects embroidered by Dame Dorothy Davenport at Bramall while her husband looked to his duties in the forest.

At the side of Capesthorne park is *Redesmere*, once famous as a floating island and now the home of a summer time spectacle, the Fanshawe water lily fete. Many villages have 'rose queens', but there can be few who have a 'Water Lily Queen'. *Siddington* church looks half-timbered at first, but we find it to be mainly brick painted to look like half-timber. Some old beams survive, and inside the roof timbers from the 14th century still exist. A treasure of the church is a magnificent rood-screen of mediaeval date, which would have been richly gilt and painted when it was first set up. In the churchyard is an ancient yew tree and a 15th century cross was restored in 1912.

By Sparkling Streams

(Peover means a sparkling stream)

KNUTSFORD has so much history that there seems to be something of interest in just about every building in the 'Top and Bottom Streets'. The 'Bottom Street' has some worthwhile hostelries, including the *Royal George* with its 18th century elegance and the *Angel* from the same period while the *Red Lion* is Elizabethan. The old *White Bear* is much restored but is probably 17th century. *The Lord Eldon* is of interest; it was called the *Duke of Wellington,* but the landlord did not approve of the Duke's support of the Catholic Emancipation Act and changed the name to that of the Act's chief opponent. Even the Chinese restaurant is in a 17th century building. Knutsford is, of course, the Cranford of Mrs. Gaskell's novel. The town still has an air of the 'elegant economy' of the Cranford ladies. The house where Miss Matty opened her tea shop is a shop today and the Mayday fair is held on the heath where Miss Betsy Barker's cow fell into a lime pit. Pilgrims from all over the world come here to see the novelist's grave marked with a marble cross.

The old chapel of the Unitarians is the place where her husband preached. It is of great interest in its own right with galleries around a central pulpit and the communion table set in the middle. It shows the Calvinist emphasis that was predominant in the 17th and 18th centuries. The Dissenters from the Church of England were well established in Knutsford when the Act of Toleration was passed by William and Mary in 1689 and plans were already made for building the chapel. It is a pleasant, peaceful spot on a slight hill with cobblestone paths amidst ferns and a pair of stairways climbing up outside. The interior is typically Puritan with clear glass and whitewashed walls.

Knutsford church was built in 1741 and is also galleried, a typical Georgian church. The brass chandelier hangs in the centre and a notice over the door tells us the seating in the church is free. When the church was first built, the local families purchased pews for themselves and the people living on their estates. As new people came to town, they found nowhere to sit. The battle to provide free seating after the growth of Knutsford in the wake of the railway link with Manchester raged in the town in the 19th century. In the spring the churchyard is brilliant with daffodils. There is a lovely Queen Anne house by the churchyard gate and a nearby garage has a plaque to remind us that a chapel of ease stood on the site before the church was built. An impressive building near the church is the Sessions House built by Harrison who designed the castle at Chester. It caused quite a stir when built, for people thought it better than many gentlemen's houses. The building was put to an unusual use in 1919 as the 'Test School' where ex-soldiers were trained for the Church of England Ministry.

The inhabitants tell you proudly that 'there's something "Knutty about Knutsford" ' and tales abound. One tells of a bear, taken into the pulpit of the old chapel. The animal placed his paw on the Bible, whereupon the bishop insisted on closing the chapel for a year and reconsecrating it. There is the story of King Canute too. They say that he crossed the River Lily here and gave his name to the crossing point. It's a possibility, but it is more likely Knut was a Danish settler here in the 9th century. The king is said to have met a wedding party coming from the church at Rostherne as he was shaking the sand from his shoes and wished them as many children as there were grains of sand (family-planning was not heard of in those days!). Even to this day sanding takes place on May-day, when coloured patterns are traced by the pavements in sand:-

> I asked Nan to wed me —
> She answered with ease
> You may sand for my wedding
> whenever you please.

May Day relics are exhibited in the library, an early may queen's dress and some crowns amongst them. The queen's crown is specially made each year in London and is hers to keep. Crowns from previous festivals decorate the windows of shops on May Day in Knutsford. There is dancing in the streets and the town is decked in finery for the day. No machines are allowed in the parade, and the queen and her retinue travel in horse-drawn landaus loaned by the Corporation of Liverpool. A rare sight today are the farm carts drawn by shire horses in sparkling brasses with ribbons in their tails. There are many traditional characters and the shoe for the old woman and her children has been wheeled through the streets since the first May Day more than 100 years ago. Higgins the local highwayman rides each year in the parade. He was a handsome man living by the heath nearby and his house still stands. He was popular at parties and dances where he danced with the finest ladies, examining their gems at close quarters, then relieving them of the jewels as they were returning home. He was active in the 18th century and met his fate after being captured after a daring hold-up in Wales. 'Jack in the green' is an ancient character in the parade, a survival of the Wicker images of Druidic times. A wicker frame is covered in greenery to form a walking tree — the ancient green-man fertility image. A later green man — Robin Hood — and his merry men, along with all our favourite story book characters are to be seen, and the 'village wedding' group is always popular.

Mrs. Gaskell's chief monument is the white tower in the lower street, set up by the architect Watts, above the coffee house which is now a French restaurant. Mr. Watts had travelled in his youth and his houses are a rare treasure, a unique heritage which

Knutsford seems to ignore. The buildings were set up at the start of the 20th century and incorporate Art Nouveau with themes from drawings made of buildings in Italy and the East. They were very much a part of their age, a laundry being used to finance the Ruskin Rooms where meetings could take place and Knutsford people could gather to discuss the arts. Even the laundry chimney (demolished in 1976) was made to look like a minaret from an Eastern Mosque. On the memorial tower are a list of English monarchs, Mrs. Gaskell's bust and a list of her books. Stones project to provide perches for birds for he was 'concerned for their comfort'.

Many of Mr. Watts buildings are in Legh Road, recalling the Legh family of Booths. The Old Hall was last used as a centre for nuclear research. Close to it is the moat of the medieval Norbury Booths, the largest moated site in Cheshire. An obelisk by the road side was made from stones from the ancient chapel of St. Helen as a focal point for the Hall. Mr. Royce, of Rolls Royce fame, moved out of his house in Legh Road after a domestic upset and set up home in a tent in the garden! The Legh Road houses are fantastic Italian villas built for wealthy industrialists who commuted from Manchester and are an important part of Cheshire social history.

Tatton Park is one of the finest houses in the country. The last Lord Egerton never married and left the estate to the National Trust, who administer it through Cheshire County Council. The house is one of the Trust's most visited properties. Things to see include the fine lakes where boating takes place and the landscaped areas, planned by Repton. He wanted two lakes while Lord Egerton would only allow one to be created. The designer got his way for today there is a second lake, a product of salt subsidence. The medieval home of the family looks like a farm house and is empty at the moment, but may be restored one day. Around it are the remains of the old village of Tatton, depopulated in the 18th century when the park was created from the village fields. We can still pick out the remains of houses in the humps and mounds around the old hall. A 'trail' of signs guides visitors around this important archaeological site and explains the life of the villagers while an old barn is being reconstructed to serve as an information centre.

The gardens of Tatton are worth a visit in their own right. New Zealand tree ferns grow under glass, and Tatton is one of the few places in Britain where oranges grow. There is also a temple from Japan on an island in a pool. The house is well looked after and we wander through the state rooms rich with paintings, stucco and furnishings. There are paintings of the Cheshire Gentlemen who met to decide if they would give support to George I or the Pretender. George won and they had full length portraits painted to commemorate the event. The library has fine books, there are brilliant chandeliers and all the requisites a great house should have. Through the kitchen wing with its interesting collections of household equipment there is the Tenants Hall where a unique museum is housed. Lord Egerton was a great traveller and collector of hunting trophies and curios. Many of his trophies (shot in Africa) form the basis of the Manchester Museum collection. Here there are trophies on the wall, curios in cases, and household items of interest. Early transport includes such items as an old fire-engine and a car with the first Cheshire number plate — M I.

Toft Hall (now a residential convalescent home) is a fine brick house which can be observed from the road. The building is Elizabethan, with a central porch tower, it is said Queen Elizabeth once slept here. The name Toft is a Danish one for an enclosure and the boundaries of the park are still visible by following the roadside banks. Similar banks are around *Tabley Hall,* which houses a boys' school with the church rebuilt when the island on which it kept company with the ancient hall started to sink as an effect of brine pumping. The collonaded hall is one of Cheshire's finest houses now administered as an investment by Manchester University. It was built in 1761 by John Carr of York, the attractive arched entrance lodge is seen from the Manchester to Chester road with a bridge in front. An old inn by this road is the *Smoker,* named after a horse and dating from Elizabeth's time.

Plumley village has a few old cottages and a rare treasure in the fields here. At the end of a lane stands *Holford Hall,* the home of Mary Holcroft, who became Lady Cholmondeley, 'The Bolde Ladie' of Vale Royal. The house is only half of its former self, standing in a moat with an interesting bridge with seats part way across. It is a wonder that any of it survives, for in the 30's it was mutilated and there were even plans to fill in the moat with chemical waste from the nearby works. The mill was demolished for firewood during a miners strike! Lady Mary was a stormy character who was determined to make her mark. For 20 years she sued her uncle to decide who should sit where in Lower Peover Church (the papers are still preserved there). The reason was of course, that she was establishing her position by taking an important place in the church.

The old church at *Lower Peover* is a gem. (Peover is pronounced Peaver.) It is half-timbered and while much of the outside is new, the inside has splendid woodwork. The old pews still survive, the central ones still bearing the coats-of-arms of the Shakerley and Cholmondeley families. The side-aisle pews were for the ordinary parishioners and have doors which open part-way up so that the occupants had to step over to get in. The centre pews would have had mats or similar floor coverings but the poorer side aisles had rushes. There are carvings of the Cholmondeley arms in the chancel and in the south chapel are interesting monuments to the Shakerleys, including one to Geoffrey Shakerley who took messages to King Charles I when he was at Chester during the battle of Rowton Heath. He found no boat to cross the Dee and rowed himself across in an old tub, his horse swimming by his side. This piece of initiative failed to achieve its object as he had promised to take the king's orders back, but the king was indecisive and the orders were not forthcoming.

The church has an old chest dug out of a solid oak trunk, said to have been here since the church was founded in 1269. It is claimed that no woman was fit to be a Cheshire farmer's wife if she was unable to lift the lid and throw it back with one hand. The lid is firmly locked today to prevent would-be farmers' wives damaging the chest or the church by demonstrating their worth! An interesting relic is a wooden hand fastened to the wall. Some say it is the hand which was hung outside the church when there were markets, others claim that it was the hand of St. Oswald, to whom the church is dedicated, which was immune from decay when the saint died because it had done so much good. However there is a more prosaic theory that it was the hand of the Byrne coat-of-arms and may have been part of a crest. The font is believed to have been here since the church was built and it has a simple cover with a counterweight to help lift it. There are old shelves on a wooden pillar on which loaves of bread for the poor were placed each Sunday from the 17th century to the 1960s. The pulpit and most of the furnishings of the church are also 17th century in date.

The churchyard looks over the little Peover Eye, a stream with a Celtic name, meaning 'sparkling water'. A large Celtic cross with a harp reminds us of the Irish ancestry of the last Lord de Tabley, a poet and botanist of the 19th century, a bramble growing on the grave was the result of his genetic experiments.

The little Victorian village school stands by the churchyard and the earlier brick school dated 1710 is now a private dwelling. There is a gate leading from the door under the church tower to the door of the 'Bells of Peover'. It is believed that the gate survives from the time when the priest's house stood on the pub site. Modern chickens living nearby have learned that they can beg drinks from the customers who sit outside. The inside is rich with brass and old woodwork. The charm of the spot is enhanced by the cobble-stone road and pavement that leads to it.

Over Peover is one of the most delightful spots in the county and we travel to it along winding lanes past the *Whipping Stocks Inn.* The way to the Old Hall and church is one of the most enchanting pieces of unspoiled old England. Only the road surface, put down during the last war, reminds us that this is the 20th century. The tower and the body of the church are of brick and date from 1811, but there is much that is older. The lovely little chapel with the monument to Randle Mainwaring and his wife is one of the most attractive in the district. Randle was known as 'the good' and when he died, he asked to be buried without much ceremony outside the church. The funeral took place in the churchyard in the way he requested, but Margery his wife had more ambitious plans for her last resting place. She did not want to lie apart from her husband nor did she want to do without a fine memorial, so the chapel was built over the graves and the fine alabaster tomb set up. Both parties were — one hopes — satisfied. However, Margery's face has been spoiled by water leaking through the roof of the tomb. Perhaps Randle got his revenge this way?

A beautiful 15th century painting in glass of the Virgin shines from the window, and more Mainwarings (of the 15th century) lie on either side of the altar. The North Chapel is 17th century and has a fine monument to Philip and Ellen Mainwaring, he died in 1650, but the tomb was set up after the Restoration. Philip has been sculpted in a suit of armour and the original suit hangs on the wall. There are some helmets from the Roundheads here too, relics of the days when they were billeted in the church.

The Old Hall, open to the public on special days, is a fine house looking rather like a fortress and was built in 1585. It is famous for its 'Magpie ceiling' and has splendid grounds with an attractive lily pond. There is an inscription above the stables telling they were built by the same Ellen who lies in the North Chapel (which she also built) as a present for her son Thomas in 1654. The stables are rich with plaster work and diamond leaded windows. Even the stalls are intricately carved in the Jacobean manner. They are a rare treasure and are well looked after. The old moat where the medieval members of the Mainwaring family had their home still survives, although the house has gone. There is a tale told in these parts of an African princess captured during the slave trade days by the son of one of the great houses hereabouts. She cursed him, saying that as she could not be queen in her land that the gentry of Cheshire would become extinct as her royal line had done. Few of the Cheshire gentlemen of the late 19th century married. Their old homes passed to new hands as the family line ended or, as in the case of the Delameres, they moved away to new lands in the expanding empire. Their fine houses, however, still survive.

The Forest Country

Here's to Cheshire, Here's to Cheese,
Here's to the pear and apple trees,
And here's to the lovely strawberries.   (folk song, Kelsall)

DELAMERE FOREST is served by a railway station linking Manchester and Chester and it welcomes visitors to its midst, providing picnic tables for walkers, snacks and in the summer there are ice cream vans amidst the trees. A museum has been opened where visitors can learn more about the forest and an old youth hostel has been converted into a centre for schools to visit and to study the plant and wild life.

It was on these central uplands that the early settlers in the county built their forts. Six hill top camps of the Iron Age exist, along with the lakeside settlement at Oakmere. The finest of the forts overlooks the rail station. Eathelfleada, the daughter of Alfred the Great, gave it the name Eddisbury — 'the happy place' — when she refortified it against an invasion by the Danes. The Iron Age camp and Saxon Burgh have left little remains other than the earthen bank, but there are remains of the hunting lodge that was built as 'the Chamber in the Forest' for the earls of Chester, its old drain looking like a secret passage. These highlands compare well with Macclesfield Forest for their wide views and from Eddisbury can be seen the modern works where Cheshire sands are dug to make tiles. The monks of Vale Royal knew this area well, they had a glass works at Kingswood which produced glass of such quality that it was sent to Westminster Hall when it was being rebuilt by the king. They fished the pool at Oakmere to provide food for the Friday table. *The Fish Pool Inn* reminds us of this, as does the *Abbey Arms Hotel* close to their quarries.

Today the roads are lined in summer by hundreds of cars, but walk a short distance and you may find your own private wilderness. Cheshire has an abundance of wild-life and those who leave the hordes of roadside picnickers — or who come in winter — will find much of interest. Delamere is still a Royal Forest and on the houses we find the monogram of the monarch who ruled when they were built. An interesting pub name is *Cabbage Hall,* reported to have been built by a tailor from the profits he made by selling the off-cuts from fabric at an extra profit — such off-cuts being known as 'cabbage'.

Tarporley is the centre of the old forest area, and *The Swan* is the meeting place for the Cheshire Hunt. The Dones were the foresters of Delamere and they have two old homes near Tarporley Flaxyards and Utkinton, both pleasant farmhouses today. There is a column in the hall at Utkinton formed by a tree from the old forest which still has its roots in the ground. The famous hunting horn of Delamere Forest once hung on the column to give authority to the foresters — it is now in the care of the Grosvenor Museum.

The horn is grasped by Sir John Done on his memorial in the church. He was given his knighthood by James I who felt that he deserved a reward for a fine day's hunting here. Next to him on the wall is his son-in-law Lord Crewe in a fine wig of the Restoration period. His wife is on the other side of the church where she lies with her sister. She wears widow's weeds and has her granddaughter who died as a child standing at her feet. Mary Crewe lived to be 90 and hers is obviously a portrait effigy. She props herself up on one arm, looking sad with an open book in her hand. Her sister's book is closed, a symbol of death. Jane was dead when the tomb was made and the effigy is clearly an idealised one. The two sisters were seldom separated during their life and they were laid to rest together. Jane was noted as a beauty and for her good deeds. A Cheshire man would tell you, 'There's a Lady Done for you', meaning a good woman.

Mary's son John is wearing an odd combination of toga-like robe and long wig. He grasps his powerful hands and casts his eyes to heaven. Two cherubs hover above him and two babes shed marble tears at his head and feet. There is also a fine screen with gates made in iron by Florentine smiths in the 16th century, enriched with gilded figures. A stately house was built in half-timber, but this is hidden under a cladding of white plaster.

> *John Done, the lord of this place*
> *was an aid to this work in every case*

was carved on a beam by a grateful owner; it was built in 1586 and juts out pleasingly into the main street, one of the most attractive streets in Cheshire.

A splendid rock cut road brings us from Tarporley to the Portal on a hill, trees overhang it and rhododendrons make a charming scene. We travel this way to *Eaton*, where half-timbered cottages cluster around a small green with the steps on an ancient cross in the middle of the road. A tree now grows from the steps. The old smithy still does some trade and we find traces of where stone was cut from the hill sides to make the foundations of the cottages. One old farm on the road to Winsford is built of sandstone and has fine mullions and transoms of the early 17th century.

At *Oulton* there is a race-track which attracts visitors from all over the world. The old home of the Grey Egertons was destroyed by fire but the park was converted to this unusual purpose, providing a finely landscaped setting for the races. The gateway by Vanbrugh still stands and has the Egerton badge or arrows above. The common is popular for picnics, and there is also a polo ground here and an old sandstone 'pound' where stray animals were taken in years gone by.

Oulton is part of *Little Budworth* and the church there looks over a small pool which gave it the name (bode worth - dwelling by water). The tower was built by the wife of Hugh Starkey, who built St. Chad's church, Over, but much of the rest was renewed in the early 19th century. The *Red Lion* pub exhibits relics of the race track while the church boasts older treasures. They include a lovely fluted font carved from fossil marble and a huge painting said to be by Caravaggio. Budworth Mill Pool is a picnic spot with a profusion of wild fowl.

Darnhall is pleasing with an old corn-mill by a brook. It was here that the last Norman Earl of Chester died while hunting; it was rumoured that his wife, Helen, the daughter of Llewellyn Prince of Wales poisoned him. Later there were troubled times when the peasants revolted against the strict rule of the abbots of Vale Royal in the 14th century. They even beheaded the unfortunate John de Bodeworth and played football with his head. The Grange was sold to Roland Hill in the 16th century and passed to the Lea family who were the ancestors of the American General Robert E. Lea. In 1824 poachers from Darnhall were sentenced to be deported for 'carrying guns at night' while hunting for their Christmas dinners on Squire

Corbett's land. They were already on board the prison ships when public outcry caused the sentence to be withdrawn on a technicality — although the statement by a witness said that they had guns at twelve o-clock, he had not said if this was noon or midnight and the men returned to their quiet village. In the later part of the 19th century the hall was the home of Verdins, the salt proprietors and philanthropists. It was demolished in the 1950s, but the wooded grounds and the former boating lake survive. Its name originates as Dern (hidden) Halle (hole) and the pleasing valley with woods and a weir is still a hidden hollow close to the concrete sprawl of Winsford's overspill estates. The 'knobs' at Darnhall were not gate-posts, but were set up to mark the spot where the former grammar school was founded in the 17th century and they used some of its stones.

Wettenhall nearby has some interesting inns out in the midst of flat farming country. No one knows who the 'Little Man of Wettenhall' was — if ever there was such a person — but his pub is here. There is an old highway known as Wettenhall Long Lane and farms are scattered about this rural region.

Whitegate is a charming and old-fashioned village with its little brick church seen from Cinder Hill, where the village bake-house scattered ashes in days gone by; it looks rather continental backed by pine trees. The school, an old cottage and a white house (which was the village inn until Lady Delamere closed it to prevent drinking after church) nestle around the village green where the maypole is plaited each year. The neighbouring *Plough Inn* was closed on Sundays until the 1960s too. The church was the 'Capela ad Porta' — the chapel at the gate of the Abbey Vale Royal. It has 14th century timber columns which have survived several rebuildings. The church was made a parish when the abbey was dissolved and the last Abbot of Vale Royal became the first vicar. We come to it through a white gate made of iron, which formerly stood in Vale Royal Park. The royal arms of Charles II were set up in the year he returned to be king. They cost £3.10.6 but the interest lies in the crown above, which is the *old* crown of England, destroyed under the Commonwealth. The new crown had not been made at the time and the artist presumed the design would be the same. The Cholmondeleys had suffered under the Roundheads and they were more than pleased when the Restoration came.

Lord Delamere of *Vale Royal* was a big game hunter of the 19th century, helping the settlement of what used to be known as the 'white highlands' of Kenya. In fact the family left this part of the world to live there, and a house called Njoro in the village took its name because the packing cases labelled Njoro were stored there before transport. King James I stayed in a specially decorated chamber as a guest of Lady Cholmondeley, whom he named 'the bolde ladie of Cheshire'. The old house stands on the bank of the River Weaver and has collected more than its fair share of legends and stories. Edward, the Royal Earl of Chester, was crossing the Channel when a great storm broke out. Afraid that the ship would be wrecked, he vowed that if he was saved, he would found the fairest and finest Cistercian abbey in England in the county of Cheshire. The boat came into port and as soon as the future king stepped ashore, fell to pieces and sank.

In 1277 the king came to Cheshire to lay the foundation stone of the great abbey, along with his Queen Eleanor. They had intended to convert the old hunting lodge at Darnhall, but the monks who came from Dore Abbey in Herefordshire were not too happy about it. They reported to the king that 'Catholic and thoroughly trustworthy men' had seen visions of the Virgin Mary in woods not far away. It was clear that she wanted the abbey built there. The king could hardly refuse. Darnhall became a grange farm for the abbey and the church at Vale Royal was built to be the longest Cistercian abbey church in England. It was, of course, a political move. The year that the abbey foundation stone was laid was also the year that the foundations of the great Welsh castles were laid. Edward was hoping for heavenly help in his wars with the Welsh and hoped to secure it by fulfilling his vow. In case there was any doubt in the Virgin's mind about the purpose, Edward invited the Bishop of St. Asaph's to lay the foundation stone.

Vale Royal had a troubled history. One abbot was killed by the vicar of Over when he was abducting Mary Hector, one of the parishioners. Another led many of the tenants into battle at Bosworth Field. My favourite story is of the nun of St. Mary's convent in Chester, who nursed an abbot back to health. They fell in love and vowed that though they could not marry, they would lie together for eternity, their joint grave being before the High Altar of the abbey. Today the spot is marked by a group of old stones placed there in 1814, including a part of a column with a medieval cross head rich with carvings of saints above it. The monument is known as the Nune's Grave. John Henry Cooke of Winsford, wrote a novel around the grave and the abbey under the title *Ida*.

After falling into disrepair and passing through a number of hands the great house is now, 700 years after the abbey was founded, being restored as a training centre for slow learning teenagers. An impressive sandstone facade was created in the 18th century as a Tudor revival. Inside the corridors, the great saloon and library were the monks' quarters, and it was developed as a great house when Thomas Holcroft obtained it at the Reformation. The south wing was rebuilt in half-timber after being destroyed by fire when General Lambert plundered the house in the Civil War; the timber gables were later faced in Victorian brick. He took everything away apart from a silver dish with the family coat-of-arms (hidden in a secret drawer) and a white pony hidden in a secret room in the wainscot panels. A white cow with pink ears escaped and was to keep the family alive with its milk for a time. A herd of the cows — probably the Dox primigenius that had been kept from Prehistoric times — were a feature of the park. A secret room is reported to be here, where the older son was taken on his 21st birthday and would never reveal its awful secrets.

Grange Lane is a winding route to *Knights Grange,* an old 17th century farm on the site of one belonging to the abbey. The brick building was high fashion at the time when Richard Starkey who recorded the siege of Malta was born there. The farm is now a hostelry in the heart of a sports complex, but the lovely lane takes us through wooded glades filled with bluebells in the spring. In Bark House, an old farm on this lane, Robert Nixon was born. He was a simple ploughboy who made remarkable prophesies, and when the king heard of him he called him to court. Nixon refused, saying he would starve if he did. They said he could stay in the kitchen to avoid this, but he made such a nuisance eating and picking at the food that the cook locked him in a cupboard out of the way. The cook was called away and Nixon was found weeks later starved to death.

Whitegate station is closed now but it has found new life, as the old railway branch which served the demolished salt works of Winsford has been developed as a country walk. Cars may be parked in the old station yard. The walk takes us past the remains of *Marton Grange* with its picturesque moat and the remains of a stone cross looking like a chair. Legend tells that a friar outwitted the devil here and he is still to be heard whistling as he tries to collect hay from the nearby sands to make a dozen hay ropes to grant wishes to those who sit in it. Marton Hole was created by salt subsidence last century.

A picturesque round tower on the main road at *Sandiway* was the entrance lodge to Vale Royal. *The Blue Cap Hotel* nearby was named after a hound who won a fortune for his owner Lord Barrymore in the 18th century while Kennel Lane and Cockpit Lane remain to remind us of sporting days gone by. Sand is still extracted here and the area boasts a fine golf course.

Hartford has some pleasing corners. The church is 19th century and has a charming monument to a sleeping babe with a bunch of lilies of the valley, looking on the font from a window sill under the tower. As Prince of Wales, Edward VII came here to stay at local houses and to have 'affairs' with local girls. Hartford has always considered itself superior. Last century a local lady complained about 'sitting in church between a soap boiler and a salt maker'. They were none other than Sir Joseph Crossfield and Sir Joseph Verdin! Hartford still has its large houses, its Old Hall is a hotel, Whitehall is Regency and has become offices belonging to the council, while the Gas and Water Boards have taken over other grand houses. Two railway lines cross here, but their stations are a long way apart — two separate companies built them and refused to share facilities. The London, Glasgow and Cornwall trains stopped on the main line station at Hartford, their only call between Crewe and Runcorn, for the convenience of a director of the Company who lived at Heyeswood close by in the 19th century. His house is gone and a modern estate covers it but the trains still stop.

The Salt Country

Our Wyches, if deprived of these,
No salt beneath the soil,
In vain to thrutch the daily cheese
Would Cheshire damsels toil.

Throughout the Middle Ages the three wyches were the only salt producing areas. Changes in production methods and improved communications took away Nantwich's trade, while developing works along the canal between Middlewich and Sandbach and by the ship canal at Runcorn to which brine is pumped from Mid Cheshire. Cheese and salt are Cheshire's traditional products and the cows chew happily besides the pumping equipment in the fields. In days gone by the railway ran through an area of small derricks at regular intervals around Lostock which pumped the brine for the nearby works. Today much of the brine is used in the production of soda ash in the great works of I.C.I.

The history of salt manufacture is fascinating and is told in the unique salt museum at Weaver Hall, Northwich, housed in a fine building which was the town workhouse dating from 1837. Exactly how the salt came to Cheshire is a matter for dispute but it is generally agreed that rivers flowing into a shallow sea in hot conditions carried the salt which built up to form thick beds because of the continuous evaporation. Changes took place and for thousands of years marl built up, then again there were changes and salt accumulated once more. Recently the Triassic beds of Cheshire salt were explored to a depth of some two miles at Pickmere in the vain hope that oil might be found in association with the lower salt beds.

The top bed of rock-salt was found in 1670 at Marbury when the land owner was looking for coal to supply the local salt works. It was this bed that had provided the 'wild brine' that had been used for centuries. The water soaked into the rocks at a distance and was fully saturated by the time it had flowed to the area of the works. No dissolution, as a rule, took place under the works but at the point where the water flowed in, the beds were eaten away and subsidence took place. Thus the Meadow Bank area of Winsford was largely free from subsidence which developed further along the Weaver, or further up the hill, where one flash is named the 'Ocean'! Early mines dug into the top bed but soon flooded and the proprietors changed to pumping brine from them until they dissolved away so much that the works collapsed.

Today the lower bed is worked at *Meadow Bank* with underground roadways covering the area of a town. There are lorries and traffic lights, taken down in parts and assembled underground in what is reputed to be the safest place in the land, for many of the nation's treasures were stored there during the war. Mountains of rock salt around it wait to be used for melting winter snow.

The salt provided the basis for wealth and prosperity and for the heavy chemical industry which developed at *Winnington* where we walk amidst towering blocks which become a fairyland at night with hundreds of lights. During the day we are amazed by the complexity of pipes with horse-shoe bends to allow for expansion and contraction and to see road-side drains steaming like small geysers. A plaque in the research laboratories recalls that polythene was invented there. The story of Winnington goes back to Saxon times, and in the midst of the works we find the Old Hall being used as a club for the management. Part of it is Elizabethan and part of it was designed by Wyatt in the 18th century. It was the home of the Stanleys and was let to Miss Bell in the 19th century. She entertained the cultural elite of her day including Hallé who founded the famous orchestra and John Ruskin the art historian, who gave drawing lessons to the pupils of Miss Bell's school for daughters of the gentry. His wife had left him for the painter Millais and had the marriage annulled as it had never been consummated. He was at his happiest in the old house and wooded park surrounded by the pretty girls whom he called 'his birds'.

When the school closed, the lovely park became a centre of industry. John Brunner and Ludwig Mond purchased it in 1872 and set up their works in the grounds. At first Mond recalled 'everything that could go wrong did go wrong'. He even had a bell hung outside his window so that he could be called at any time if there was trouble. The works flourished and became one of the foundation stones for the vast I.C.I. complex. Good housing was provided for the workers along with sports and recreation facilities, but no pub was allowed in Winnington! We remember Mond by the gifts he gave to the Tate Gallery, an extension was built to house them. Brunner's name is kept alive in many gifts to Cheshire, including a library at Northwich and a guildhall at Winsford. The other philanthropists who made a fortune from Cheshire's salt and are remembered by their gifts were the Verdins who gave infirmaries and technical schools to the district. The Winsford school became one of the largest comprehensive schools while the Northwich one evolved into the Mid-Cheshire College.

In Northwich we find the true heritage of the salt. Old photos show the town at the turn of the century with narrow alleyways, buildings leaning at odd angles, some have sunk so much that they are reached by steps leading down, others have been raised to allow them to sink again and are reached by steps leading up. One customer at the *Wheatsheaf* must have rubbed his eyes and wondered if he had drunk too much for when he came out, his horse and cart had vanished into a hole in the road!

Someone had realised that older half-timbered buildings resisted subsidence, and could be lifted, while those of brick simply fell into ruins. Soon the town was rebuilt in half-timber construction. Nixon, the Cheshire prophet, said that Northwich would be destroyed by water. Had they not tipped thousands of tons of waste ashes and the like into the craters and continued to raise the levels of the roads, the Bull Ring area would have been a lake today. No building in the town centre is joined to its foundations, pubs like the *Crown* keep their beer at ground level — its cellar is some 30 ft. down now. The timber frame allowed the buildings to be raised on jacks and placed on new foundations, as the town sank they could be lifted up to the new road level. Each trader tried to outdo the next and as this was the period of romantic escapism and of the 'arts and crafts movement' they based their buildings on historic ones, but adapted them to create a fantasy idea of what an old English market town *should* have been. There are carvings of 'Olde England' turrets fit for a fairy tale princess, cavaliers support the roof of a bank and the town crier and night-watchman keep an eye on shoppers in this conservation area.

The fine old church at Witton stands above the town — it took its name from 'Wych Tune' where the salt workers lived. It is a stately 16th century building, with a magnificent ceiling said to have come from Norton Priory, but in fact it is 10 ft too narrow. It was clearly made for the church as it has the initials of William Venables (lord of the manor) and 'barrows' (baskets) in which the salt was drained, carved on the bosses. Carvings from the church are on show in a small open air museum at Vicarsway Park nearby, along with other items of local interest. There are pleasant walkways by the Dane with the impressive viaduct carrying the railway above.

Winsford became a development area in the 1960s and much new housing attracted overspill from Liverpool and Manchester. It has lost much of its old character but there are some 19th century timber pubs by the bridge, overlooked by the timber-framed church built for bargees on the Weaver. They call Winsford 'Dark Town' because it once only had one street lamp by the bridge. They also point out that there's only one house in Winsford and that's a public one. The truth is that Winsford is merely the bridge-point between Over and Wharton. When they linked the two to form an urban district in the 1880s, the name was chosen as a neutral one.

The Mayor of Winsford is also by courtesy 'Mayor of the Ancient Borough of *Over*' and has two maces, a 17th century one for Over and a 19th century one for Winsford with the Prince of Wales' coronet instead of a crown, reminding us that he is also Earl of Chester. Over received its charter around 1300 from the abbot of Vale Royal but was never very prosperous. An old tale tells how the mayor visited Altrincham once upon a time and as he felt rough after his journey, he called at the barber's for a shave, and full of his own importance, informed the man that he might tell his customers that he had shaved the Mayor of Over. Unimpressed the barber pointed out that he was being shaved by the Mayor of Altrincham.

An old rhyme tells of

The Mayor of Altrincham and the Mayor of Over
One's a thatcher t'other's a dauber.

No mayor of Over, however, suffered the indignity of one Mayor of Altrincham who stayed in bed while his breeches were mended — he only had one pair! On the other hand, the mayor of Over had the legal right to disturb the middle one of any three pigs in his borough and lie down in its place!!

The 19th century church of St. John has a touching monument to the mothers and children who died in a great fire in the Over cotton mills. The mill owner's house — Over Hall is the local council office today. Close by is the old cross, almost unique as it has a prison cell under the steps. Tradition says that it marks the spot where St. Chad's church once stood. The devil, angered by the fact that few souls from Over were coming his way because of the excellent use that was made of the church, determined to stop this. They say he intended to drop it on Nantwich church, but was frightened by the monks of Vale Royal who rang the abbey bells. The people of Over prayed and the angels carried it to rest where it stands today, in a valley overlooking the flashes. They say St. Chad preached here after crossing the Weaver on one of his journeys and baptised converts in the little brook that flows by the church. It is probable that some early settlement existed here and a fragment of a Saxon cross is in the church. Today a single cottage, formerly the *Bluebell Inn* keeps it company; in days gone by, it would have provided stables and refreshment for parishioners who made the long journey from the scattered farms of the parish to attend church.

Hugh Starkey, shown in armour, who built the church in the 16th century, has a fine brass on an altar tomb, and an inscription tells that he was the Gentleman Usher to King Henry VIII. The epitaph was made during his life and as he knew he would die after 1500, the Roman Numerals MV wre inscribed for someone to complete the date of his death when it happened. No one ever did. In fact the knight depicted is *not* the builder of the church at all. For when the church was altered, Hugh's epitaph was placed at the feet of his father's effigy and his father's epitaph, which once ran around the stone, was removed. You may still see the brass nails that held it. Enlarged in the early years of this century there is a Jacobean holy table, and a small door at the east, said to be where lepers received communion, but more likely giving access to a vicarage or vestry long since demolished. There is a priest's room above the porch with Hugh's coat-of-arms, a play on words showing a 'stark' (stork) and an 'aye' (adder). A holy water stoup in the porch and a cross outside were smashed by the Puritans. 'Drunken Barnaby' came here in the 18th century and commented:-

I came to Over, O profane one,
And there I met a Puritain one,
Hanging his cat on a Monday
for killing a mouse on a Sunday

The Weaver was made navigable from 1721 onwards and the offices of the Weaver Navigation Trustees is in Navigation Road in Northwich. They gave the Duke of Bridgewater the inspiration for his canal and they produced some engineering marvels themselves. The Anderton Lift which carries boats from the Weaver to the Trent and Mersey some 60 ft. above, was considered to be one of the 19th century wonders of the world. The swing bridges in Northwich and at Acton Bridge are built to float on pontoons, partly to counter subsidence and partly to relieve the weight problems. They are cantilever constructions and the oldest electric swing bridges in the world. Problems solved on the Weaver helped in the construction of the swing bridges and the swing aqueduct on the Manchester Ship Canal. There are double locks at each stage of the Navigation with a narrow one for the old sailing 'flatboats' and a larger one for the seagoing ships which still make their way to Northwich from the continent to take goods away from Winnington.

There are boat yards in Northwich where boats are still repaired from time to time and where Lawrence of Arabia worked on the production of a top secret radio vessel during the Second World War. The boats are launched sideways into the river, but the industry had declined in these days of motorways. In its busiest days the Weaver Navigation contributed to the Industrial Revolution by showing the way to the canal buildings and helping the growth of trade. Salt was exported from Liverpool and used in part as bartering material in the slave-trade. The slaves were taken to America to work in the cotton fields, while the cotton came back to Liverpool to be spun in Lancashire's mills. The boats that took the salt to Liverpool, returned filled with imported goods, or came back filled with coal that they collected via the St. Helens Canal. They were seldom empty, it was said that they arrived black and went away white.

There are three churches built by the Trustees for the bargees to ensure that they did not waste their day off if they were away from home on Sunday. One at Weston Point, one at Winsford and one on *Castle Hill,* Northwich, showing Christ baptised in the Jordan in its stained glass, a particularly apt picture in a waterman's church. Castle was the site of the Roman fort of Condate, guarding the fording point where the Weaver and Dane join. Up to the 18th century the water was only a couple of feet deep here where the Dane deposited sand-banks, today a dredger is continually seen there removing them. The Romans may have worshipped Condatis, the god of the waters meet, before crossing the river and used his name for the settlement. Lead pans, said to have been used by the Romans for the production of salt, have been found here and a vast quantity of Roman material, including a unique helmet, a pottery kiln and metal working hearths have been traced in excavations. The name 'Castle' probably derives from 'castra' — a Roman Camp.

There is a wealth of industrial archaeology in the Weaver Valley, old salt works, boat yards and the like and warehouses where the salt was once stored. One of them near Moulton with timber columns looks like a vastly outgrown baronial Hall. Propellors and anchors from the bottom of the river have been dredged up and set close to Winsford High Street in a new park. At Acton Bridge the *Legh Arms* is a 'mock Tudor' pub looking like a pantomime set, with a display of knots used by the boatmen. The Weaver and the Navigation Channel run side-by-side towards Frodsham, where the Marsh Lock joins the Navigation to the Ship Canal.

The Ingram Thompson works at Wincham, by the Trent and Mersey, are the last works to make salt by the old 'open pan' process with vast iron pans in sheds with open roofs to allow the steam to escape. Close by the *New Inn* was built to replace the Wych and Devil which slowly sank as the ground subsided. The landlord moved his bar up a floor at a time until he had only the attic left and then abandoned it to the waters of the flash. (A flash is the local word for a pool created by subsidence).

The Heart of Cheshire

BY THE village green at Bostock there stands an oak tree with two brass plaques which state it was planted in Queen Victoria's Jubilee year and marks the traditional centre of Cheshire. It replaces an earlier tree which became unsafe after centuries of growth. The villagers of Davenham would disagree with this claim for they say their church spire is at the county's centre. Exactly how they work this out no-one knows and it would take a considerable amount of detailed survey work to prove either correct. Indeed boundary changes have now altered the shape of Cheshire so much, there should be some contender for the honour.

Davenham Church is, for me, the sign that I am nearing home when I travel this way along the road that takes traffic from Manchester and North Wales around the town of Northwich, but the old tree will always be known as 'Middle o' Cheshire'. The impressive spire is of a church which goes back to Saxon days. The name of the village incorporates the old name for the river on whose bank it stands. 'Daven' is the name of a Celtic water spirit whose name is also found in varied guises throughout Europe from the Danube to the Dee. The meandering river is a charming place for walks or fishing.

Davenham village is an interesting little place with charm. There is a stone fountain shaped like a lion's head under a canopy on the hill outside the village, and the 18th century *Bull's Head* still has its old inn sign and cobblestones, with a mounting block in the forecourt. Further along the road out of Davenham we pass the pools of *Billinge Green*, formed by subsidence from salt workings in the 19th century and now a favourite place for fishermen.

Close to Billinge is *Shipbrook* where one of the Norman barons built his castle, but nothing of that survives today, while beyond is the wild open land of Rudheath, where outlaws gathered in the Middle Ages when it was a sanctuary for criminals. A 'garden suburb' of Northwich was developed on the edge of Rudheath between the wars with garden bakeries at *Gadbrook* to provide jobs for the wives of the men who worked in Northwich and Lostock. It was described as 'a Paradise' when first built. King Street the great Roman Road from Middlewich to Warrington runs this way as straight as an arrow.

Bostock was created in the 19th century as a 'model village' for Canon, Colonel and Captain France-Hayhurst, three brothers who lived in the Old Hall here. The Hall is now a school for maladjusted children but the village they created remains. The houses are all very much alike, set in large old fashioned gardens so that the tenants could produce their own food. There is an old smithy and an old pump under a roof by the side of the road. The road through the village is one of the loveliest roads I know with its overhanging trees. Peckmill is in a pretty valley close by with the stream running under the mill house.

The road takes us into *Middlewich*, an unpretentious little town, which has seen a new road destroy some of the older parts, but offers a valuable relief to the centre. The church is dedicated to St. Michael and sits on a small hill. There were two battles here in the Civil War but all is peaceful now. The church has old carvings on a low screen that separates the nave from the chancel. They may have been imported from the Continent, but the poor-box of 1862 was obviously made for its position by the door. A brass panel of 1591 recalls Elizabeth Venables who is shown with her family in prayer. The first Baron of Kinderton was reputed to be a bastard son of Hugh Lupus — Earl of Chester, who took his name from Venables in Normandy. The remains of his castle survive close to Kinderton Hall. Under the tower the 17th century screens that once surrounded the family chapel are now set, richly painted with coats-of-arms of the various families to which the Barons of Kinderton were related. Their crest, a dragon eating a child is above. A story tells of how one of them killed the beast at Moston, (where the name Dragon's Lane survives to this day) as it was eating a child. From then on:-

> *A dying dragon bathed in gore,*
> *Which e'en in death an infant tore,*
> *In arms he thenceforth proudly bore*
> *Emblazoned on his shield.*

In fact the poet was wrong for the dragon was the crest, not the coat-of-arms on his shield. Outside, as statue of Christ carved in sandstone in the Middle Ages sits in a niche in a buttress, blessing the passing traffic. Here too we find the memorial stone which reads:-

Some have children some have none,
But here lies the mother of twenty one.

A more amusing epitaph to a local character was removed by the church authorities. It proclaimed:-

Here lies Humphry Suddler,
When he was alive he was a fuddler
Now he's gone you need not cry,
He wants no drink, he's never dry.

The church looks across the little river Croco and the canal by its side to the site of Roman Salinae. The name is translated as 'the salt pits' and several Roman salt making furnaces have been traced. There is evidence of a long settlement of timber buildings lining the King Street for about two miles here. In the library—one of the few modern buildings in this old town, can be seen some of the objects found in excavations. Newton Hall is a charming building with a brick wing of Elizabeth's period on the side of a larger Georgian House. The Elizabethan wing was no doubt intended for demolition to be replaced by a matching wing which was never completed and the house stands today a curious mixture of styles.

Middlewich is a pretty town
Seated in a valley
It has a church and a market cross,
And eke a bowling alley,
All the men are loyal there,
And pretty girls a plenty,
So up with the King and down with the Rump
There's not such a town in Twenty.

So sang the Cavaliers in the Civil War when they took refuge in the church. Middlewich has tended over the years to be oblivious to her charms, and it takes some searching by the visitor to find them, but unlike Northwich and Winsford, the place has retained much of its historic character. When they made the new boroughs, Middlewich expected to join Northwich and Winsford. In fact it was joined to Congleton, but the character of the place has more to do with the market and country towns of the Congleton borough than it has with its traditional allies in the salt industry.

Middlewich is a canal town and no mention of it would be complete without reference to the canal cruises which start here and the lock-side pubs which provide convenient resting places. Today they are patronised by pleasure boat enthusiasts rather than by bargees, but they are an important part of the heritage of this place where the Trent and Mersey is joined by a branch of the Shropshire Union.

>*Proud Warmingham, poor people,*
>*New church, old steeple.*

This couplet tells much about one of the most out of the way villages in the county. I know of few places where the sign posts show the way, but are followed by 'first right' or 'second left'. The church has an 18th century tower and a 19th century body. The spot is a pretty one, with the weir of a mill on the Wheelock close to it. Warmingham is one of those scattered places so typical of Cheshire that has no real village centre, but it does attract visitors at night, the 19th century Grange is now a night club.

A charming place on the road from Winsford to Crewe is *Church Minshull*. From this village came the family of the last wife of John Milton, the blind poet had been unlucky in love—his *Samson Agonistes* is a bitter reflection of this. Elizabeth Minshull married him, looked after him and returned to Cheshire when he died. The village has retained much of interest, the old village smithy is still here, though it now repairs tractors instead of shoeing horses and the mill has survived too. It spent a time producing electricity before its wheels ceased to turn. Close to it is the Mill House, a splendid timber framed house sometimes called 'Toad Hall' (t'owd hall). A building by the church has a porch room on columns above the door and the church has the date 1702 picked out in blue bricks on the tower. The old half-timbered building was demolished because of disrepair and neglect to be replaced with this Queen Anne structure. Fred Crossley was worried that this spot might be ruined in the 40's It has seen some new housing and a rather unfortunate modern silo looking like something from outer space, but it is largely unspoiled.

Wades Green close to Minshull has the distinction that General Wade who was in charge of the army during the 1745 rebellion, and George Wade the commander of the 'Fighting Temeraire' immortalised by Turner, were born here. *Ashbrooke* is a lovely stream crossed by a bridge on the road to Winsford amidst wooded farmland.

Moulton was formerly a single street village, whose residents worked in the mines and salt works of Winsford. It has grown since the war, becoming a prosperous suburb of Northwich and Winsford. It is of great interest to those who study old customs for it is the home of the 'Moulton Crows'. There are those who claim the dance has origins in a far distant past, while others claim that it was invented by a Victorian dancing teacher. The villagers dressed as crows dance round a human scarecrow while live pigeons fly out of his clothes, the farmer comes with his gun to shoot the pigeons but shoots the crows instead. The dance survived until the 50's and was revived in the early 70's but it is now, sadly, a school child's performance that we see. *Stanthorne Lodge,* a fine Georgian house in the fields, gave Dickens the story of the jilted bride who lived with her wedding breakfast for many years. He immortalised the lady as Miss Haversham in *Great Expectations*. The house stands in a good 18th century landscape setting and is now a farm.

Dwellings by Water

THE NAME *Great Budworth* translates as dwellings by water, and this old village on its hill top overlooks the lovely reed-fringed mere, a haunt of wild fowl and sailors whose yachts make this a picturesque scene. The old *Cock O'Budworth* is mentioned by Drunken Barnaby in the 18th century. He found the ale so good, two servants had to help him to bed. With its cobblestone forecourt and its stables (now converted into a room for meals) the pub looks much as it must have done when he came here.

Close by Georgian *Belmont Hall* houses a school—the moat of an earlier hall is in the grounds. We turn off by a little roof over a spring to climb the hill into the old village where every house has an interest. Some cottages were built for the Arley Estate by John Douglas, who also designed the ivy clad *George and Dragon*. The pub bids us welcome in a charming way. Above the door we read:-

> *As St. George in armed array*
> *Did the fiery dragon slay,*
> *So might you with might no less*
> *Slay that dragon drunkenness.*

There are other inscriptions around the pub and we still find one or two of the rhyming sign posts set up by Squire Warburton in the 19th century.

St. Mary's is a fine 15th century Perpendicular church, not unlike its daughter church of Witton in Northwich whose tower is seen in the distance. The same builder was responsible for both towers— Thomas Hunter—who left his name on Witton.

Inside the church is a battered effigy of Sir John Warburton who died in 1575. He keeps company with oak stalls dating to the 13th century—the oldest woodwork in any Cheshire church. Sir Peter Leycester, the Cheshire historian, is buried here, he detailed much of Cheshire's history and collected many old documents. Besides writing the monumental *Historical Antiquities* which contains a large section on Cheshire, he records an interesting moment in the church's history, when in 1559, by order of Queen Elizabeth, the wooden image of the Virgin was taken out and burnt in the vicar's oven'. Rich woodwork still exists in the church roof and there is an abundance of carvings, including monkeys, a fox and Eve with the serpent. There is an altar stone too with its crosses where a medieval bishop blessed it. The old church has stocks by the gate and a 17th century brick schoolhouse is decorated with hearts and diamonds picked out in blue brick. A sundial over the door would remind pupils not to be late. The village has a variety of house types, including some timber buildings with brick infill, (known as brick-nogging). A cottage dated 1706 reminds us that half-timber continued to be the standard method of building for many years after brick became available elsewhere.

Marbury Hall on the other side of the mere once housed one of the finest collections of classical art in the country. It was a splendid building looking like a French chateau. Its park was the temporary home of many Polish refugees who settled in Mid-Cheshire after the war. The Country Park is open to the public and is enhanced by old and well-established trees. It also has a small swimming pool — a reminder of the days when the Hall was used as a prisoner of war camp — they created it as a work project. The story of the Marbury Lady and her ghostly white horse tells of the strange foreign lady who came back with the owner of this house from his travels and refused to attend church. When she died, she asked that her bones stay at the house — which was agreed. Eventually a successor took the bones to Budworth and they were buried there. From then on the ghostly figure was seen until the bones were returned, to be kept in a chest under the stairs. They were taken again to the church by a third successor, but again the hauntings started. The lady was finally put to rest under a rose bed in the garden where she is — one hopes — quite happy. The horse of the story won a bet by running all the way from London to the Hall non-stop. In the excitement no one watched the horse — which drank too much and died. How the two became linked is a mystery — but there are still people who will not travel this way at night in case they meet the lady on her horse.

At *Arley Green* is a picturesque timber-framed village school with tall chimneys and a row of tall chimneyed cottages keeping it company by a little brook. *Arley Hall* has belonged to the Warburtons for five centuries, it was rebuilt in the 19th century when Roland Egerton, a grandnephew of the previous Lord inherited it and took the name of Egerton-Warburton. He laid out the gardens which are a delight today and are open to the public. They are much as they were in the 19th century, with one of the oldest herbaceous borders in the country and an avenue of ilex trees trimmed to resemble columns. The hall and private chapel are available to parties of people, but the fine cruck barn of the 14th and 15th century is open to all as the visitors' tea-rooms.

Marston is a village under water, rather than by water, for here old mines have collapsed and brine subsidence created pools. *Wicham* too has seen houses sink under the waters. The Adelaide Mine was the last to go and the remains of the machinery at the top of the mine shaft can still be seen peeping above the water where grebes now swim and nest. The Tsar of Russia came here in 1844 to dine in the mine by the light of ten thousand candles as he was guest of the Royal Society.

Pickmere has something of the seaside about it as the mere has been developed for leisure and there are boats and fairground rides. *Barnton*, developed after the Industrial Revolution, has an older origin. Its famous tunnel on the Trent and Mersey canal brought prosperity in the 18th century, while the growth of the chemical trade in the 19th century prompted further growth with new development after the war. There are some quaint 19th century corners of Barnton but much is new here. It is known as 'Jam Town' for its inhabitants are said to be too poor to eat anything but 'jam butties'.

Weaverham is on the other side of the Weaver and the old village is now swamped by modern estates. The old church of St. Mary belonged to Vale Royal Abbey, which had a prison here and a grange at Hefferstone. The church is like St. Chad's at Over, another Vale Royal property and the same mason's marks are found on both.

The church has a rare treasure, a holy table made by Chippendale, with elegant claw and ball feet. One of the most interesting items is a sandstone slab with a head and shoulders and what look like horns. A number of theories have been proposed, but none are conclusive; it has been identified with pre-Christian religion or an attempt by a local to immortalise the image of Queen Eleanor when she came here for the founding of Vale Royal Abbey wearing a double steeple head dress. It may well have been used in some black magic ceremony and represent the Devil!

In the 1590's Weaverham church was in the care of the Reverend Edward Shalcrosse and was the most notorious church in the whole province of York — since nearly everything that should have been done to comply with Elizabeth I's protestant rulings had not been, and the vicar was described as a 'common drunkarde' who had been found in a ditch after one of his frequent visits to a local alehouse! Weaverham remembers another eccentric vicar too, the absent-minded Charles Spencer Stanhope, who returned from his honeymoon and left his bride behind on Acton Bridge Station! The vicar wrote sermons on loose unnumbered sheets and would often lose the order, or would change the hymn part way through the service, confusing the poor man who operated the barrel organ and had to announce the tune that had been set on the organ.

A romantic tale tells of the daughter of Mr. Heath, who made a fortune through the slave trade and purchased stately Hefferstone Grange. She fell in love with the garden boy, but Mr. Heath did not approve. Eventually she eloped with him riding to a Gretna Green wedding on a bamboo bike (apparently they were common before the First World War!) She returned to live with her village boy in an old thatched cottage here. Hefferstone today is a property of the Hospital Board. Warrington Corporation had a sanatorium there providing a home in the fresh air for T.B. sufferers in the 20's and 30's before clean air acts and pasteurised milk made such places redundant. It is a gracious house of 1741 with rich plaster work inside. Weaverham has also some charming half-timbered cottages, and an old sandstone grammar school. The *Hanging Gate* inn with its mounting block takes its name from the old name for this part of Weaverham, 'Weaverham Gate' or 'Yate' indicating a high road. It stands on the A49, the Roman Road from Warrington to Whitchurch.

The Mersey View

THE HILLS that look out over the Mersey have been a defence in days gone by, but are now a pleasure to climb. The Iron Age occupants of *Helsby Hill* looked out on a wild untamed wooded country where they built their earthen rampart around the camp there. The water level was some ten feet higher then and the waves of the Mersey washed around the foot of the hill. The river made an ideal highway for water traffic and the fort could observe all this activity. Two more camps are at Bradley and Woodhouses, silent witnesses to the Iron Age in these parts, while flint tools found at Frodsham tell of people who settled here long before that.

On the hill side at *Halton* Romano-British farmers had an enclosure consisting of huts which were excavated as part of Runcorn's development programme. The hill above may have had some significance in very ancient times and it is worth the climb to see the old castle, now a ruin but still Crown property, as part of the Duchy of Lancaster. A hotel built into the ruins where we may rest after climbing the hill was built as the Court House in the 17th century. It has the arms of George III hanging outside the sandstone hotel. The castle was held by the Parliamentarians in the Civil War. Before that it had served as a prison and as a hunting lodge for John of Gaunt. It sits on an imposing little hill which was selected shortly after the Conquest by Baron Nigel who took its name. There is a fine Georgian vicarage and a little building next to it built as a library in 1733 by John Cheshyre, a wealthy lawyer who endowed it with £12 per year. It contained 40 leather bound books on the classics, history and theology. The vicar is still responsible for one of our earliest public libraries.

When *Runcorn* was declared a New Town, Halton was declared a conservation area; it keeps an aura of the past while overlooking the roofs of the new town. There are sandstone houses of the 17th and 18th centuries in the village and a row of sandstone terraced houses on the hill. A further bonus is a fine panorama of the Mersey with the ship-canal leading to Manchester and the bridges linking it with Widnes. The railway bridge has a castle-like tower on either side and reminds us that Aethelfleda had a castle where its foundations are. The new road bridge with its single arch and the road suspended on metal cables is a wonder of the 20th century. Once Runcorn was a health resort and was called Monpelier, now the chemical works of the district give it a rather different air. A modern wonder is the great shopping complex called 'shopping city' with scores of shops under one roof. The busy town has 'expressways' and a unique 'busway' service.

This busway takes us to the most unexpected place. In the heart of this new town we find a park with a ski-slope and other sports facilities and an ancient Priory. A great house which stood here until the 1920's replaced a Tudor house of the Brookes family, which in turn was formed from part of *Norton Priory*. The remains were excavated as part of the New Town scheme. They are just below Halton Hill, where the baron who founded the Priory lived. The remains include the foundations of the church and cloistral buildings. An undercroft has Norman work and a fine Norman door-way. Lovely arcading was found behind the brickwork of the later house and all has been carefully restored. There are old stone coffins with carved lids; one group is believed to be those of the Duttons of Dutton. A sad group appear to be those of a father and three children who may have died from plague. Here too were found some of the most important tiled floors to survive from the Middle Ages. They have been lifted, and will form the main feature of a museum. Norton Priory is the largest excavation carried out on any monastic site to modern requirements. It is a rich legacy in this 'new town'. The old village of Norton is now being investigated by archaeologists. *The Tricorn* is a modern pub on the site of an ancient moated manor house. Parts of the moat may still be seen, while the Shaw museum tells of Runcorn's later history.

The town has attracted new industry, but still retains many old links. Rocksavage has given its name to one of I.C.I.'s works, close to the magnificent house built by the Savages who rest in Macclesfield church. John Savage died at Frodsham Castle the same night that his fine house at Rocksavage was burnt in the Civil War. Both remain in name alone. Frodsham Castle is remembered only through Castle Park where the Vale Royal Council meet in a 19th century building. A few walls of Rocksavage survive around a farm overlooking the river Weaver and the Navigation Channel.

Runcorn is a place with definite canal associations and though they are now disused, the flight of locks which carry the canal down to the Mersey are of interest. At Weston Point, the church built for boatmen on the Weaver which joins the Mersey here now serves as a parish church for the local community.

Ashton by Sutton is a picturesque place with an early Georgian church (made new after bomb damage in 1940) with old monuments on the walls and a little cupola which holds a bell that once belonged to a ship on the river. There is an old stone with a hollow into which vinegar was poured to disinfect coins as they passed from hand to hand in the plague. The old Hall has been demolished, but there are remains of the estate buildings, the wall with the entrance lodge and a moat where an earlier Hall once stood.

Thomas Ashton from the Old Hall commanded the Royalists until his defeat at the battle of Middlewich. The most remarkable pos-session of this parish is an exquisite chalice and patten of the 14th century, the only church plate to have survived the Reformation in the county.

Frodsham church sits on a hill looking out over the river and the lowlands that were once flooded. People moved down into the valley during the Middle Ages leaving the church in an isolated position. The church has Norman work in the arcades and a group of Norman stones have been preserved. The round arches of the arcades and clerestory windows are attractive with some capitals and bases. A carving of Christ in Glory built into the tower is all that remains from the church that was mentioned in the Domesday Book. There are two 17th century holy tables in the church and an 18th century monument to one of the most noteworthy clergymen.

Francis Gastrell was vicar here from 1740 to 1772 and as was the custom of those days, he employed a curate to conduct the services while he lived far away from the parish. He lived in the house Shakespeare built at Stratford and became so annoyed at visitors looking into his garden to see the mulberry tree the playwright had planted that he had it cut down. He quarrelled with the authorities at Stratford over the payment of taxes and before he returned to Frodsham he took a final, spiteful revenge. He demolished New Place, the house that Shakespeare had built for his old age.

Frodsham has one of the widest main streets in the county and on a market day it is alive with shoppers. The 17th century *Bear's Paw* has seen many a market day and served many of the customers with refreshments. The gabled sandstone inn has its old stable yard where the stage coaches would call. Close by are old houses built onto the solid rock from which the road was carved. The 17th century Old Hall is now a hotel, mellow with old oak, brass and antiques.

The village of *Daresbury* has a 19th century church rebuilt on the site of an older one, of which the tower dated 1110 survives. The date is believed to have been recarved in error as the tower is 16th century. Inside is a Jacobean carved pulpit and rich old woodwork has been reused to form panels behind the altar. A fine sentimental marble monument on the wall shows Henry Byron mourning with a child in his arms over the body of his wife — a girl of just 18.

Daresbury vicarage was the birthplace of Charles Lutwidge Dodgeson in 1832. Dodgeson grew up to become an Oxford don and it is in this guise that he is shown in a window kneeling in prayer at the nativity. He has a companion, a little girl in a blue dress with long flowing hair, while St. Francis and a wolf are also there. The little girl is none other than Alice of Looking Glass and Wonderland fame; her companion is better known by his pen name, Lewis Carroll. The characters he created are here in stained glass, even the Cheshire Cat grins from this Cheshire window. Close by a case made from old wood removed from the church last century contains a book with the names of lovers of his books from all over the world who contributed to this window memorial to the writer. The old vicarage which the writer described as

> *An island farm, midst fields of corn,*
> *Swayed by the wandering breath of morn*
> *The happy spot where I was born,*

has gone now, but this part of the world has many such island farms to delight the visitor; the poem is on a plaque on the site. Close by is a wonder of the twentieth century in the Nuclear Physics Laboratory. *The Lord Daresbury* is a first class hotel for those who need refreshment or accommodation.

The charming *Holly Bush* at *Little Leigh* is an old inn that has been in the same family for generations—it is an almost perfect example of a brick nogged house of the early 17th century, complete with its ancient fireplace and 'Heck', that is a small wall opposite the front door to make a porch and keep draughts from the fire. The original front door has been bricked because the building was made into two cottages at one time. There are other old cottages close by and in the summer traction engine fans assemble here to demonstrate the machines in use at the turn of the century.

Stretton takes its name from the Romans—it is the 'Street Town', and two Roman roads meet here by the 19th century church. The remains may be picked out in the fields close by. *The Cat and Lion* is believed to have originally been the *Cuer de Leon* named after Richard I, but changed by locals over the years. The sign tells us that

> *The Lion is strong and the cat is vicious,*
> *My ales are good and so are my lickers.*

Appleton has a church of Queen Victoria's day and a thorn tree said to have been cut from the Glastonbury thorn which sprang from Joseph of Arimathea's staff to tell him that that was the place where the Holy Grail should rest. Children used to dance around the bush on 29th June. The tradition no doubt had its origin in pre-Christian days, as a form of mid-summer fertility rite, perhaps linked with tree worship. The thorn was decorated with paper and ribbons for the ceremony known as Barning the Thorn. A pagan rite that continued in these parts is the fire jumping in the village of *Alvanley*, a purification rite which has its origin in Viking, and earlier traditions. Alvanley itself is a pretty place of great charm.

The souling play is still performed in *Antrobus* and surrounding villages at Hallowe'en time. It is performed around the hostelries of the district, with the traditional mummers, characters of St. George, the Black Prince and so on. The horse's skull used for the play is centuries old and has its origin in Celtic religion where it would be linked with the Goddess Eppona. The theme of the play is the victory of good over evil. In the play St. George has become King George, the Black Prince is a black painted prince, and the horse has three legs. Children used to travel from door to door in Cheshire singing the souling song up to the 1950's, for food or coppers which later became ousted by the 'penny for the guy' tradition which needed considerable less effort.

By the Ship Canal

THE traveller who comes to North Cheshire might well stop to wonder if his eyes are deceiving him. For at times amongst the fields or at the end of a street, a great ship is seen sailing peacefully by. Of course this is Ship Canal country. It cost £15 million to build this modern marvel when it was opened in 1894. The Egerton family had great interests in the building, and there are paintings of the canal being dug and other canal souvenirs at Tatton Hall. The canal is 35 miles long and its total length is the Customs Port of Manchester. The little river Gowy vanishes into twelve foot wide pipes to travel under the canal and to be syphoned into the Mersey. One hundred and thirty men died while working on the canal construction. The canal cut through the ancient site of *Wilderspool* (wild deers pool) where the Romans had their settlement of Veratinum with great timber workshops. One building excavated in 1966 was 150 x 100 ft. When excavations were carried out, the ships sailed by only a few yards from the dig and a Roman lead coffin was washed out from the banks. Veratinum had potteries, glass works and metal works. Today a brewery stands on the site where the impressive swing bridge links Warrington New Town and Stockton Heath. Wilderspool was an industrial settlement, and recent research has disproved the theory that a fort stood here.

At *Thelwall* the motorway rises above the river and canal on an impressive roadway reaching skywards; this concrete wonder of our own day gives an excellent panorama of the district. We read on the black and white *Pickering Arms* a quotation from the *Anglo-saxon Chronicle* that Edward the Elder founded a 'city' here in 923. The 'city' is but a small village today, with an 18th century Hall and a few cottages. There are other traces of those days in the names of Norton, Sutton, Aston (Easton) and Weston, around a place called Stockholm - conjectured to be the first stockade of the Teutonic settlers. The Pickerings of the Pickering Arms were lords of the manor and the inn with its cobbled yard and an old fire-place was their manor house.

Stockton Heath has a small shopping centre with a sculpture made from the remains of a forge where Dick Turpin's horse is said to have been shod. A canal-side pub, the *London Bridge* has some other canal-side buildings of interest close to it. The road from Northwich comes to Stockton Heath through a cutting in the sandstone at *Hill Cliff* where prehistoric remains have been found- it is a picturesque piece of road close to a chapel where Cromwell worshipped.

The canal-side drive to Grappenhall, where Bronze Age men

buried their dead, is pleasant. The old church has an old inn with dark beams and the village stocks to keep it company. The village street still has its cobblestones and gas lights—an old fashioned village in the heart of Warrington!

The church tower has a carving between the west window and the ringers window of a cat with a decided grin. Is this the Cheshire Cat? Or were cats proverbial when this church tower was built? The date 1539 is on one of the pillars, but the foundation goes back long before then. A huge font almost like a bath tub with a carved arcade around it is Norman, and was found last century buried under the floor. Sir William Boydell, who died in 1275 is shown in the fashion of his time, cross-legged with his hand on his shield wearing a surcoat over chain mail. Since the effigy was made, it has been moved out of the church into the churchyard, taken to Warrington Museum for safe-keeping and returned here in 1874. A modern brass recalls Sir Thomas Danyers of Bradley Hall who rescued the Black Prince's standard from the French at the battle of Crecy. His daughter and heiress Margaret married Sir Perkin Legh and the estate of Lyme, given in recognition of his bravery, passed to the Leghs. Grappenhall has some fine medieval glass including a lovely Virgin (in the organ screen) shown with long flowing hair and a robe trimmed with ermine and pearls. An ancient oak chest is in the church again, after a period in Warrington Museum.

There are some picturesque places in the Grappenhall district. The canal provides pleasant walks along the tow path and there are pleasing old buildings scattered about among the over-spill from Warrington, not to mention impressive 'high level' bridges cantilevered over the Ship Canal.

Walton Hall is 19th century. Its grounds have been taken over by Warrington as a park where there are gardens with rare plants, and a children's zoo, along with leisure facilities and tea-rooms in the Old Hall and bands play there in the summer.

Lymm and Warburton were proverbially linked—'I'll tear yer Lymm from Warburton' they said in a fight in days gone by. It was the same as saying 'Limb from limb' and perhaps was derived from the days when the two parishes shared the same clergyman. Today it has been accomplished: Lymm remains in Cheshire, but Warburton's old church near the Ship Canal with its timber-framed walls and air of the past has been taken into the care of Greater Manchester. Lymm church keeps the story of an old crone who always stole water from the church spout because rain water was better for washing than pump water. Her neighbours and even the parson tried in vain to stop her, until one stormy night when she came to place her bucket so that it could fill with rain water from the church roof, a skeleton hand came down the spout, snatched the bucket from her and hit her on the head. Hand and bucket then vanished up the spout.

The church looks over to the delightful lake called Lymm Dam, created when the main Warrington road was improved in the 19th century. It was thought better to build a dam than a viaduct and the ravine here became a lake. The pleasantly wooded slopes are an asset to the district and there is a lakeside walk known as the 'Bongs', an example of Cheshire dialect, in which vowel sounds are changed. In this case 'O' for 'A', most outsiders would of course say 'Banks'. Cheshire folk say 'Etts thee pays of a pleet', where others say: 'Eat your peas off a plate'. There is a unique Cheshire vowel used instead of 'O'. A cross is reputed to mark the earliest coming of Christianity to these parts but what we see today is mainly 17th century. Restored in Queen Victoria's time, it has a plaque dated 1897 to commemorate her Diamond Jubilee. Three sundials remind us to 'save time', 'think of the last' and 'we are but a shadow'. The cross dominates the market square, and may well have replaced an earlier one destroyed by zealous Puritans; it keeps company with the village stocks.

In a valley we find the remains of a slitting mill, carefully excavated when the zone was made a Conservation Area. We can trace where the mill wheels once turned and where the machines stood which cut sheet iron into thin strips for making nails and barrel hoops. It is first recorded in 1720, but had been in use for many years before. The gorge in the sandstone is a pleasant park with a little cave once used by the mill as a store.

Lymm is said to derive its unique name from 'Hlime' — a roaring brook. There are those who claim it has Roman origins, an odd stone in the church has been claimed to be a Roman altar and the footprints of prehistoric animals have been found here in the sandstone. The gorge is carved out between foliage-covered sandstone cliffs 100 ft. high, the cross sits on sandstone steps carved from the living rock and old stone houses gather round it. Today it attracts people to settle in the district since it has a good shopping centre and lively social activities. The canal district is probably one of the early settlement areas of the county, since several dug-out canoes of indeterminate date have been found — estimates range from the Bronze Age to Anglo-Saxon times. Bronze Age burials and other early artefacts have been found. In this part of the county, the Mersey, the Ship Canal and the Bridgewater Canal flow close to each other, and a pleasant way of exploring the area is from one of the boats for hire on the Bridgewater.

An attractive village not far from the canal is *High Legh*, which gave its name to many old Cheshire families who had their origins here. An old rhyme about the Cheshire families tells us that there were:-

> *As many Leghs as fleas, Crewes as crows,*
> *Masses as asses and Davenports as dogs' tails.*

A 17th century writer called Cheshire 'the seed plot of Gentility' and at High Legh we feel the presence of those great families of long ago. Swineyard Hall is a black and white house with part of the moat still containing water and has interesting old farm buildings. Two branches of the Legh family lived here, one in the East and the other at the West Hall both of which were demolished. The gracious 18th century High Legh Hall has pleasant gardens. The old chapel was built in 1581 to be the private chapel of the East Hall. It is a splendid old structure with wooden columns and some old stained glass including the Madonna riding on a crescent moon. A bomb landed nearby during the war blowing the glass from the windows but it has since been restored. The chapel is rich in oak panels and old woodwork. The present church is sited where the West Hall chapel stood until destroyed by fire in 1893. There is an ancient feel to the place with its timber walls. The village contains an old cross and the stocks, along with a group of stones which tradition says will work their way to the surface if buried.

A copper beech tree near the chapel was planted by Robert Moffatt who was garden boy here in 1813-14 and returned with tears in his eyes as an old man to declare that it was in this village that God had revealed himself to him. Moffatt became a missionary and it was his descriptions of Africa and his work there which made his son-in-law David Livingstone decide against going to China as a missionary and set his heart instead on the Dark Continent. Today Robert would hardly know the place. The Old Halls have gone and modern private houses cover much of the old estate. They have spacious gardens and here and there old trees, that he must have known, are left

The New Lands
North of the Mersey

WHEN they gave Cheshire's 'dormitory' areas to Manchester and Liverpool to create new counties, they gave Cheshire a part of Lancashire that has much in common with the Cheshire Plain in return. The main towns, Warrington and Widnes are riverside places, they are old established Rugby League towns and in 1975 they met in the Cup Final at Wembley for an all Cheshire 'Derby'.

Warrington was settled even before the Romans had a crossing point here and set up their workshops where the Wilderspool Brewery is now. Veratinum they called it and its industries set the pace for what was a 'town of pretty bigness' in the 17th century. Today it produces wire (the Rugby team is known as 'the Wires'), leather, soap and much more, not to mention the distinction of having three breweries and a distillery. They make their own vodka here and offered a prize of a week in Warrington to a contest winner recently, making the second prize two weeks in Warrington! This belittles the town whose artesian wells provide the origins of the breweries but there is also much of interest here. Typically northern with winding streets, it has a strange claim to fame as 'The Athens of the North', a title it shares with Edinburgh.

The title was earned by a brick building almost dwarfed by a statue of Cromwell who looks towards the Parish Church where old cottages have plaques telling of his action therein in 1648. The building is the Warrington Academy, built in the days when Oxford and Cambridge would not accept anyone who was not a member of the Church of England, for those Dissenters who were amongst the leading intellectual lights of their day. Joseph Priestley who discovered oxygen was there, as was Marat, the French Revolutionary, known as 'the friend of the people' who advocated the extermination of all Royalists until he was stabbed by Charlotte Corday in 1793 in his bath. Other great names associated with this place are Kay who invented the flying-shuttle, John Howard the prison reformer and Dr. Percival, a pioneer of sanitation in Manchester who founded the Literary and Philosophical Society there, and a host of others who helped to make England the great nation that it was in the 18th and 19th centuries. It is the most remarkable in that the academy was only in existence from 1757-86. It is sad and neglected today amidst less aesthetic aspects of the 20th century; pubs, a cafe and traffic lights keep it company and there are those who would get rid of it altogether.

Warrington Parish Church stands some distance from the town centre exhibiting a quaint charm. Inside a show-case displays some objects from the past. Its dedication to St. Elphin, said to be the oldest dedication in the county, and the presence of a 'sacred well' caused speculation that the area might have been sacred in Celtic times. The mound of a Norman castle and the well were investigated by archaeologists. England's third highest spire is capped by a weather vane of 1860 said to be plated with coins raised by an appeal for 'a guinea for a golden cock'. There are magnificent monuments to the Boteler family. Their old home at Bewsey is a shadow of its former self, but is to be restored as an historic centre. Having attracted more than its fair share of legend, excavations are expected to reveal much of its past. There is something amusing about a brewery town being the property of the Botelers who lived at Bewsey Hall! The chapel of the South Lancashire Regiment in the church is now exiled in Cheshire; Cairo, Egypt and Suez Streets recall their action against Napoleon in Egypt which earned them their sphynx badge. They have their own museum in the town.

Warrington continues the northern tradition of 'Walking Day' when the members of the various churches parade around the town wearing their best clothes as it is a traditional holiday. The fine Georgian church in the centre has an odd structure with a clock at the top of the tower which is the property of the corporation not the church. An Augustinian friary gave its name to Austin's Lane. Remains are to be seen in the museum which is housed in the library building, the first to be financed out of the rates anywhere; an achievement for a brewery town in the days when brewers tried to prevent library development because they felt that the poor would spend their time in the warm library rather than spend money in warm pubs. We come to the museum time and time again to see things we have missed, delightfully Victorian, 'the sort of museum that belongs in a museum'. It would be tragic to see this collection re-displayed in modern settings; here is a link, like the Academy, with the days when Warrington linked industry and intellectual development and thinking men cared enough to assemble this collection for public edification. There are Prehistoric and Roman antiquities, ethnological collections, fine porcelain, stuffed animals and birds, memorabilia and a treasury of geological specimens.

Thomas Patten made a fortune from copper works here and built a magnificent house with Corinthian columns which now serves as the Town Hall. Soap making developed in the tobacco shortage caused by the American War of Independence. Tales are told of secret hiding places in the works to avoid tax payments. The Sankey Brook Canal was the first true canal and industries associated with it prospered in the late 18th century. Today its prosperity lies in the motorways which link in the area, giving the New Town Development Authority their motto 'Crossover'. It is a shopping centre with the *Barley Mow*, an old half-timbered pub preserved by the new market.

North of Warrington we find *Winwick*, known for its mental hospital and memories of the Civil War. Cromwell's men pursued a party of Scots from Walton le Dale. Under the Duke of Hamilton they took up a position at what was to become known as the Red Bank after more than 1,000 men died when they 'turned like beasts at bay' on their pursuers. Five years earlier in 1643, Colonel Assheton repulsed Royalist troops here and it is claimed that a thousand years before in 642, King Oswald died in battle against the heathen Penda here. The arms of a fine Celtic cross carved with figures believed to represent his martyrdom are preserved in the church.

There is the entertaining tale of the Winwick pig which is carved on the church tower. He is reputed to have moved the stones each night to this spot when work started on building in a different part of the village. They say the village was named after the pig's call 'win-ick' as he moved the stones. More likely he kept company with a statue of St. Antony who lived with a pig in the desert though the saint has gone, his companion still remains. The church sits on a little road-side knoll. Inside are fine effigies and brasses including one to Peter Legh with priest's vestments over his armour, showing that he 'took the cloth' after a life as a knight. Once this was the richest parish in England. The Reverend John Hornby commissioned Pugin to rebuild the chancal in 1848 giving it a much higher pitch than the nave. It looks now as though some disaster has destroyed the nave roof. He later endowed nine daughter houses out of his stipend.

Besides the picturesque village, Cheshire gained more modern marvels including the Nuclear Research Laboratories and Remand Home at *Risley* and the air-base at *Burton Wood*. It was once the largest American Air Base in Europe and many local girls became 'G.I. brides' in the post-war years. The first American in Burton Wood was the incumbent of the church here who returned from the Pilgrim Fathers' settlement in the 17th century.

Widnes, Runcorn's sister town, is a workaday town with chemical industries which do not help to provide pleasing scenery, but is not without charm in a northern industrial way. Ironically in this place is a pulpit built into the churchyard wall for outdoor services. Paul Simon wrote his popular song 'Homeward Bound — I wish I was ...' while stranded on Widnes Station one night. It has the oldest railway company dock anywhere which was first known as Widnes Docks around 1840. North of the town is the oldest railway viaduct, built by George Stephenson for the Liverpool-Manchester line, the world's first public railway and close to it is the memorial to Mr. Huskisson. the M.P. who stepped in front of the *Rocket* and was killed here. The old transporter bridge has gone, having been replaced by the great suspension bridge in 1961 when it was the largest in Europe, but it is remembered by a mural in the town centre. The name Widnes originated as 'wide-nose' but this is nothing to do with the inhabitants, it recalls a wide nose of land in the estuary. During the war scientists worked out the complex chemistry of uranium in the library here, enabling the first atom bomb to be made.

Next to Widnes is the attractive village of *Hale*. We lost Hale near Altrincham to Manchester in 1974 and received in its place this Hale which retains much of its period charm. In 1844 Mrs. Carlyle wrote to her husband 'I had some twenty miles of driving through very pretty country, and saw a 'beautifullest village in all England' called Hale'. While this might be a little of an overstatement, there will be few who will dispute the charm of the whitewashed cottages, a lighthouse converted to a home and the 18th century church with an older tower. John Middleton has an iron rail around his epitaph. He was known as 'The Childe of Hale' and grew to be 9ft 3ins tall in an age when royalty surrounded themselves with unfortunates like giants and dwarfs. Gilbert Ireland of the local manor house took him to the court of James I. He disgraced himself when involved in a wrestling match with the king's favourite by winning the match and dislocating the favourite's thumb. Having thus displeased his royal, if unpredictable master, he was sent home with £20 to die here in 1623 at the age of forty five.

Somehow the new lands over the Mersey fit the character of Cheshire more than the 'dormitory towns'. They, along with the industrial areas that went with them, were unlike the rest of the county. The new lands are of similar character and scale to the rest of Cheshire; small villages and average sized towns, giving a good balance between industry and agriculture, local in character and tradition.